BALINTAWAK ESKRIMA

BALINTAWAK ESKRIMA

Filipino Fighting Art

Sam L. Buot, Sr.

"It's all in the left hand"

www.TambuiMedia.com
Spring House, PA USA

DISCLAIMER

The author and publisher of this book DISCLAIM ANY RESPONSIBILITY over any injury as a result of the techniques taught in this book. The reader is advised to consult a physician as to his physical condition to assume any strenuous training or dangerous physical activity. This is a martial arts book and trains dangerous techniques that can cause serious physical injury and even death. Practice and training requires a fit and healthy student and a qualified instructor.

We do not offer any legal advice. Any statement which may be interpreted as a legal advice is pure opinion of the author and has no basis in law. He is not a US trained lawyer. In the event of any incident using your training as a martial artist, exercise your Miranda Rights. Remain silent and consult your attorney before you say anything to the cops or the people around you. Any self-incriminating statements uttered by you will be used against you in court.

This book was first copyrighted in 1991 and again in 2007 by Samuel L. Buot.

Copyright ©2014 Samuel L. Buot, Sr.
First published February 28, 2015 by Tambuli Media

ISBN-13: 978-0692312995
ISBN-10: 0692312994

Edited by Mark V. Wiley
Design by Summer Bonne

TABLE OF CONTENTS

Part 5 Balintawak interpreted: Application of Balintawak

Part 6 Balintawak in Transition

DEDICATION

From the Eagles Nest

(Pugad Lawin)

This book is dedicated to the masters who shared their knowledge, unknowing of the significance of their contribution to the cultural heritage of a proud Filipino people. We all owe the art to the Great Grandmaster Venancio "Anciong" Bacon, whose genius and skills never saw much of the product of his work during his lifetime. Like many geniuses of their art – Mozart, Van Gogh and Beethoven – they died poor but their genius prevails and outlives their mortal bodies. Also deserving credit are my other teachers, Atty. Jose Villasin, my compadre and tutor, together with his partners, and Teofilo Velez, also a student of Anciong, a teacher, a foot soldier of Balintawak, ever faithful to its cause. Among my early tutors was my cousin Teddy Buot, heir apparent to Anciong until his departure for the US in 1974. To the intrepid Balintawak Warriors both living and dead, who from the eagles nest flew in quest of the "impossible dream," and planting the seeds of Balintawak worldwide. Many students have missed their chance to bloom through early demise.

I also dedicate this book to longtime faithful students with special mention of Craig Roland Smith who has spent countless hours and fortune for the propagation of the art, taking all photographs and videos for this book and my current students Adam Tompkins, Bart Vermilya, Ryan Buot, Nick Thompson, Rob Casquejo, Thiel Ruperto, Leonard Meuerer, Carlos Sevilla, Sal Banuelos, Audie and Gallant Betita and Danny Sevilla and other unnamed and unaccounted past students, friends and family who have placed faith in my passion; special mention goes to my stable-mate Bobby Taboada for his steadfast loyalty, *FMA Informative* publisher and editor

Steven Dowd for his support, loyalty and encouragement and to Tambuli Media publisher Dr. Mark V. Wiley, for his faith in the project. To Sal Banuelos, who has contributed greatly to this book, especially in the picture taking, Audie and Gallant Betita, for demonstrating some techniques. Finally, thanks to my son Ryan Benjamin Buot, who has been my sounding board for new ideas; my sparring partner, critic and innovator of new ideas.

This book would have never been finalized without the loving patience of an indulgent and loving wife, Menchie, who may have wondered about the time spent on this book and the free lessons given to pass on and preserve the art. I never viewed Eskrima as a source of livelihood and as a means of making money. The whole family may have also wondered whether this has been a childish pursuit of juvenile pleasure or whether this is true passion and devotion to an indigenous Filipino art.

Students of the art may not realize the value of its history, the accumulation and compilation of techniques from the masters even from other students over a lifetime of study and some innovations I have created and originated. I have paid a lot of money and time to learn them. One single technique will be well worth the price of this book, a price I would have eagerly paid to learn.

In closing here, I would like to share one of my favorite proverbs.

He who knows not and knows not that he knows not: he is a fool—shun him.
He who knows not and knows that he knows not: he is simple—teach him.
He who knows and knows not he knows: he is asleep—wake him.
He who knows and knows that he knows: he is a wise leader—follow him.
—Unknown

DANIEL 5:11 A MAN IN WHOM IS THE SPIRIT OF THE HOLY GOD: IN THE DAYS OF THY FATHER SHOWED: LIGHT, UNDERSTANDING, WISDOM-LIKE GODS WISDOM, WAS FOUND IN DANIEL, SO MADE MASTER OVER MAGICIANS, ASTROLOGERS, SOOTHSAYER CHALDEANS. DANIELS CAPABILITIES: INTERPRETING DREAMS, SHOWS HARD SENTENCES, DISOLVING DOUBTS, DEMONSTRATION DOES PROBLEMSOLVING. DANIEL CALLED BELTSHAZZAR WILL SHOW THE INTERPRETATION. 1 CORINTHIANS 1:18,19 Word of the cross is POWER OF GOD. IT IS WRITTEN "I WILL DESTROY THE WISDOM OF THE WISE. ICORINTHNS 1:6,8, We speak wisdom, yet a wisdom not of this world is GODS wisdom Contained in a mystery.

OWNER   LEONARD ELWOOD MEURER.

TESTIMONIALS

Since there is paucity of serious reading materials on eskrima, this written work proved to be a good contribution not only to the Filipino martial arts but to other Filipino performing arts as well. This is also a noble attempt to help in the preservation of an indigenous knowledge that took generations of Filipino artists to develop. The author, Sam Buot, is not new to eskrima. For decades he immersed himself into eskrima and we are grateful now, that he is finally sharing his experience and codifying his profound thoughts on this matter. The author's insight on Balintawak Eskrima, the essence of this work, is hard to come by in this contemporary sports-oriented eskrima world. Eskrima as a whole, belongs to humanity and ought to be shared with many people and for many generations in the future to appreciate. It is aptly said, *verba volant scripta manent*—spoken words fly but written words stay. So having a book like this on eskrima is a great literary contribution indeed. What we are about to read is, of course, just a small but significant fragment of an intangible cultural heritage from this side of the vast Pacific. This work partly describes what we Filipinos are made of and what we can do. And since this is a cultural matter, we Filipinos are proud of this work.

—*Ned Ra. Nepangue, MD*
Cebu City 30th July 2014

In knowing Sam Buot over the years I have found it a joy to watch him executing Balintawak Eskrima with smoothness and precision which leads to perfection. His abilities as a teacher are among the highest of qualities. Often we have talked about the history of Balintawak, wherein Sam draws from his own experiences. This book by Sam Buot which has been put together from personal experience and research is a book that even some Balintawak practitioners will have their jaws dropping, scratching their heads and thinking how come we did not know this. For anyone that gets this book it will be a book that is a treasure trove of knowledge and a book which will be considered one of the best if not the best book on Balintawak.

—*Steven K. Dowd*
Arnis Balite, *FMA Informative*

I want to extend my greetings and good wishes to you, Sam Buot, as a part of the Balintawak eskrimador family. Your skill descendants and followers will have utmost pride and respect in you, for they were taught not only your eskrima excellence but also the will to survive. As one of your colleagues in the social environment, I am proud knowing in person as my compadre and sparring partner during the early Balintawak years. You are one of the best eskrimadors I have ever crossed sticks with. On behalf of the Kritters Group Balintawak-Marapao Aggression System (KGB-MAGGS) I would like to express my gratitude to you as author of this book in keeping Balintawak on the forefront of eskrima. Daghang Salamat Pare Sam.

—*Dr. Ben Marapao*
Cebu City, Philippines

My sincere greetings to Sam Buot on his book on Balintawak Eskrima. It is great to see that he has researched the people and the history of an outstanding Filipino art developed by the late, and phenomenal Grandmaster Venancio "Anciong" Bacon. Having been a student in Michigan of the late Manong Ted Buot, who was G.M. Anciong's dedicated student and instructor at the Balintawak Club in Cebu, I can clearly see the genius of how G.M. Anciong had developed the techniques of his art with extreme accuracy and timing. With Sam's Balintawak background and first-hand experiences, his book will keep the legacy of the art alive and well-remembered.

—*David Hatch*
Attributive Martial Arts
Canton, Michigan

Grandmaster Sam Buot was introduced to me by my dad Atty. Jose Villasin as Sam Buot was a fellow attorney with the same interest in the Balintawak Arnis Eskrima. The year was 1978. I recall Sam Buot started his Balintawak lessons from my dad Atty. Jose Villasin. Since then I started hearing more about him. Sam Buot showed great interest and was very sharp in picking up his lessons so quickly. My dad introduced one lesson after another since Sam absorbed it so fast and understood his lessons quicker than his other students. He thought it may be because he is a lawyer or he is just gifted in understanding things.

Sam Buot has been very loyal to my dad and to the art of Balintawak. They met regularly at the club house, our home, Velez' backyard, or at Atty. Buot's home with GM Venancio Anciong Bacon and GM Teofilo Velez, Bobby Taboada, Nilo Servilla, Chito Velez, Ben Marapao, Nick Elizar, Nene Gaabucayan and the rest of the Balintawak International Club family of which my dad was the president. Atty. Buot was elected vice-president. Because of Sam Buot's sincerity and loyalty, my dad did not withhold any secrets and techniques from the abecedario to the most polarizing training method he called "groupings" —a method and concept devised by my dad to internalize, visualize, memorize and master the reflexive moves and responses to any offensive strikes from any direction. This has been considered a high point in a student's training. There were more offensive techniques which were never taught except to a few, and Atty. Buot was one of them.

Atty. Sam Buot has the proven integrity, training and experience. Furthermore, it has been the relationship between the GM Bacon, my dad, his teachers and that he showed his loyalty, confidence, sincerity and respect that I recognize and congratulate Atty. Sam Buot for his book. More power to you Grandmaster Sam Buot!!!

—*Ver Villasin*
May 30, 2014

I may be a bit partial with this book since the author is my uncle. Sam Buot has devoted a large portion of his life preserving, promoting and chronicling the history of Balintawak and the lessons he learned from my dad, Grandmaster Anciong Bacon and his other teachers. His journey has been one of growth, innovation and discovery without abandoning the true essence of the Anciong Bacon Balintawak legacy.

Because of his avid pursuit and passion in keeping the Balintawak legacy alive—the techniques, history, stories and anecdotes about this indigenous Filipino martial art will be preserved for posterity. Sam Buot first held the stick through dad and shared his first Balintawak moments in our backyard in Cebu. His lessons were far and few in between due to his studies at Silliman University. It was through dad that he was introduced to Mano' Anciong as an observer of the big boys. The old man was related to our family and he showed deference to both my grandfather and to Uncle Sam's father. Thus, Mano' Anciong also had a soft spot in his heart for my father Teodoro A. Buot. I know this book will be an excellent coffee table conversation piece and a source of information and history for Balintawak enthusiasts. I wish you well for this wonderful endeavor.

—Melissa Buot-Favazza

During my years as a student of the art of Balintawak, there were three instructors that aided in my development. The following were instrumental in helping shape my learning and progress in the art:

1) Atty. Jose Villasin awakened me to Balintawak in 1967; 2) Teofilo "Tatay" Velez educated me with a solid and full understanding of *Balintawak*. He also endorsed me to Manoy Anciong Bacon; 3) Manoy Anciong Bacon elevated my keen awareness of the nuances of the art. I will always remember his wise words: "Keep your composure," "Adapt and overcome the threat," "Sniff me out," "Move the body," and "Keep playing."

Today, as a member of the senior generation of the *Balintawak* Community, I would like to offer my congratulations to Grandmaster Sam Buot for the completion of his book, and wish him the best of luck in spreading and disseminating this knowledge.

With Humility,
—Sir Bob Silver C. Tabimina

FOREWORD

Grandmaster Sam Buot is a true student of Balintawak Eskrima. He is one of the few survivors of the original students of the late Great Grandmaster Anciong Bacon who died in 1980. His techniques and knowledge are direct from the masters. If there is anyone who can teach them to the world, it is Atty. Sam Buot.

I have known Atty. Sam Buot for the last thirty some years. He is a lawyer by profession and a very successful real estate businessman in the Philippines. On top of that he is a fellow Cebuano whom I met while he was under the private tutelage of Great Grandmaster Venancio "Anciong" Bacon, Grandmaster Jose Villasin, and my beloved mentor, Grandmaster Teofilo Velez. Sam was totally immersed in studying and experiencing the unique and original Balintawak moves and techniques by these Grandmasters, known to all Balintawak students in the "70s" as "The Team". I was then an instructor and I always looked forward to be assigned to train with Sam, a man of affluence, for the selfish reason that I could also eat the food and drink imported liquor that the Grandmasters were enjoying.

GM Buot has been very helpful in building up the names of the masters of Balintawak and his fellow *eskrimadores*, highlighting their achievements. It was GM Buot who helped me settle in Phoenix, Arizona when I first came to the U.S. from New Zealand and Australia before finally moving to North Carolina.

Now in his late seventies, he wants to leave a legacy behind for future eskrimadors. Congratulations to Atty. Buot for his book. It will be a handbook for eskrimadors worldwide.

Grandmaster Bobby Taboada

FOREWORD

How does an eskrimador insure his legacy? Some form large organizations and teach seminars the world over. Others put their personal history and their art down in writing. Sam Buot, the author of this book, did just that—and there was so much to share, it took him 20 years from start to finish! The book you now possess is the work of decades of preparation. Little by little Manong Sam wrote down his stories, remembrances and the nuances of every technique he could recall. I received a copy of his then 400+ page PDF and contacted him immediately to turn it into a book. And what a task it was! I mean how do you reduce 400 pages of text into 300 pages of text and images? With nimble editing and clear vision. Many sleepless nights, weeks even, tuned into nine months of reorganization, a dozen photo shoots, editing and reediting and refining. At 78 Manong Sam showed how tireless a warrior he is, putting many younger writers I have worked with to shame. And we are grateful for his effort. After all, Manong Sam is the eldest living disciple of the late Anciong Bacon, the grandmaster and founder of Balintawak Eskrima.

In this dense volume, Sam Buot takes the reader on a deep journey into the belly of Balintawak Eskrima, laying the foundation with a look at Philippine martial history before jumping right into the formation of the Balintawak style in the 1950s. That was an important yet volatile time in Eskrima history, especially in Cebu, where entrenched eskrimador clans like the Saavedra, Romo, Ilustrisimo, and Canete families tried to stake their claim of prominence. One name rose from these times, and that is Anciong Bacon and his Balintawak Eskrima, an art that has had many fabled masters, including Bacon himself, as well as his top disciples Jose Villasin, Teofilo Velez, Ted Buot, Delfin Lopez, Bobby Taboada and Sam Buot, among others.

After enticing the reader with an intimate discussion of the history of eskrima and Balintawak's place in it, Buot tells the stories of the great masters of the art. He was a participant observer and is uniquely qualified to set the true history. His narrative style is compelling and makes the reader feel like they are by his side hearing tales of old first hand. We feel like we are in the old clubs, watching the masters perfect their skills. Their poverty and dangerous living quarters bringing us chills and a close look at the many rare historical images reveals the conditions. We are then treated in several chapters to Manong Sam's eskrima secrets: the principles and strategies he has developed and perfected over a half-century in this dynamic art.

While no book can hope to be "complete," this book by Sam Buot is comprehensive and does more than any other to establish the legacy of Grandmaster Anciong Bacon, Balintawak Eskirma and the book's author, himself. I am proud to have worked on this project with Manong Sam and I am honored to call him my friend.

—Dr. Mark Wiley
Publisher, Tambuli Media
February 09, 2015

INTRODUCTION

The art of Eskrima stick fighting is indigenous to the Philippines, developed and practiced for centuries. Until the 1980s, however, the art was hardly known outside the Philippines. In a polyglot archipelago like the Philippines, eskrima was also known as pagkalikali, panandata, didya, kabaroan, kaliradman, sinawali and arnis or arnis de mano in Luzon. It was also known as eskrima, olisi, garote or baston in the Visayas. In Mindanao, it has been known as kalirongan, kuntao or silat. In the Pre-Spanish Philippines it was also called gilas. The term kali, while quite popular in the United States and Europe, was a term unheard of by me as a student of the art the past half a century.

The Philippines has 87 languages and dialects, 16 of which are major languages. Words and terms vary from province to province. This is explained by the fact that there are 7,107 islands spread over the archipelago further broken up by the mountains and natural boundaries. Centuries back, tribes and kingdoms, sometimes warring, isolated them further from each other. There was no national identity until the islands were consolidated by the Spanish invaders. Thus, development of a national language did not happen until the last century. I prefer and use the Cebuano terms for forms and techniques in the art of Eskrima, as this is the language in which I learned the art in Cebu.

In my personal research of the etymology of the word in the 1980s, I have concluded that Cebuanos may have borrowed the word eskrima from the French word *escrime*, meaning fencing and from the Spanish word *esgrima*, meaning swordplay or fencing. The etymology of the word may be by an attempt of 17th and 18th century Filipinos to sound sophisticated by borrowing words from the colonizing European (Spanish) invaders. It was also possible that the Spaniards gave it its name or escrime or eskrune by the French for fencing. Regardless, the word eskrima is the accepted generic Visayan word for Filipino martial art. It has now been adapted worldwide as the origin of the word. Eskrima now is synonymous with the terms arnis and kali; arnis is more predominantly used in other areas in Luzon and kali is more predominantly used in the USA than in the Philippines. I have heard of some strained explanation of the etymology of the word kali, which I am ignoring.

Eskrima is a complete martial arts system. It is not only stick fighting for which the art is known and famous for but does in fact include other weapons fighting, most especially knife fighting and defense and bare hand combat emanating from the fist and hand fighting methods called panuntukan, suntukan, buntalan or banatan, sumbagay and bunutan. There is also the grappling systems known as bugno', dumog or layug. Basically, it is pure self-defense and, until recently, it was never considered a sport. There are no limits to the target area or the seriousness of the injury inflicted. There is no concept of foul blows. In fact, in Balintawak Eskrima—the subject of this book—foul blows are mastered into a science.

The birth of Eskrima is indeed humble. In the early years of self-defense clubs in Cebu, the members were usually specialist in their own respective fighting arts. Some were boxers, others were wrestlers and some were knife fighters or weapons specialists. At that time in the history of the art, eskrima was practiced by law enforcement officers, labor union leaders and enforcers, thugs, hooligans, criminal elements and the "Great Unwashed," the proletariat and in Filipino, we called them the *bakya* crowd. I remember seeing a peddler wearing a *salakot* (farmer's head gear). Jimboy called him his *salakot* student Ramon, and a baker also named Ramon. No last names to remember. He also had a *bibinka* (rice cake) maker named Istan, none exactly belonging to the elite of society. Many of them were known only by their first names.

These were the poor people who wore wooden clogs and pushed carts to markets. The original members of the self-defense clubs were not exactly members of the social elite or of polite society. As a young lawyer, I admit, I was embarrassed to be associated with the group. We practiced in secrecy and for the most part, it was not something we bragged or talked about. It was something I learned and practiced mostly for survival in a violent society, disarmed by the dictator Marcos. That is all hindsight. As a nationalist, however, I also found the art to be native and indigenous to the Philippines. It was something Filipinos could call their own; thus my keen interest in the art. Besides, during Martial Law in the Philippines, when owning a gun was punishable by death, eskrima became the better option for self-preservation.

Although rattan is the common training weapon in use today, sometimes Philippine hardwood known as kamagong is used. It is a heavy, hard and sturdy weapon. Sometimes bahi was more commonly used. Bahi is taken from the buri tree, a palm tree with the outer trunk of which is very hard, dense and fibrous. This is a favorite of Philippine martial artists and fighters since it is more abundant and cheaper. The hardest wood in the Philippines is called the mangkono or the Philippine ironwood. Although this is the hardest wood in the Philippines, I have not heard of it used as an eskrima weapon, probably because it is very rare and expensive. It is most probably an endangered species. This is usually used as a substitute for lignum vitae, claimed to be the hardest wood in the world found in the Bahamas. Takesha Okuma at Camp Courtney Okinawa claims that the hardest wood in the world is tiga found in Sibuyan Islands, Philippines.

The bladed weapons in the Philippines include the sundang, baraw, pinuti, bangkaw, baraw, karambit, lagaraw, sundang, palamenko, daga, kris, laring, kalis, barong, gunong, golok, kampilan, gayang, pita, punyal, itak, banjal, bangkon, bankaw, lahot and panabas. The tameng was the term they used for the shield. Of course, the Batanguenos are world famous for their fan knife or balisong, which is an entire fighting art in itself.

The bladed weapon is very common on Philippines streets. It is the cheapest form of deadly weaponry with the dearth and scarcity of guns. Knife fighting or more accurately knife assassinations are the more common way of avenging a grudge, settling a dispute and of attacking or killing a foe. Thus, the art of knife fighting and defense is intrinsic and core in the Filipino culture. In rural Philippines, the ubiquitous bolo or machete was the farmer's choice. It was a utility blade used for chopping wood, cutting grass, coconuts or used as a weapon in the event of confrontations or settling of disputes. Usually, a family had a special self-defense bolo which was slimmer and longer called the pinuti. This emanates from the root word puti, and pinuti means, *made white*. Since the weapon was so shiny and clean, thus, the evolution of the name.

The balisong or fan knife is known worldwide is made in the province of Batangas and it is also known as the Batangas knife. Those sold worldwide or made elsewhere have locks on the wrong side of the flip-cover. This was probably deliberately done to confuse the unknowing user, thus keeping its secret use and methods to themselves. There would never be mastery of its use with the flip-lock on the wrong side of the blade. Needless to say, blades, bolos and knives were also used in crimes of robbery and murder.

In Cebu, where I came from, the entire districts of Basak and Mambaling were lined with blacksmiths and blade smiths that forged and created fancy fighting knives as well as the commercially used bolos or sundang and the fancier pinuti. What we call knife fights are more of assassinations, since the attack was usually in response to an affront, conflict or wrong that many poor and down trodden people resort to rather than drag and settle in court that was expensive, unjust and frustrating, usually tilted and favoring the rich and powerful. The oppressed poor mock the justice system, ridicule the courts and scoff at death. They settle their wrongs their own way, usually with the cheapest form, knives; thus, the culture of knife fighting or knife assassinations.

Eskrima and Arnis especially involve the use of weapons. Yet, despite common perception, Filipino fighting arts on the whole include bare hand combat strikes on hitting points with the use of hands, feet, knees, elbows, head butts, biting and further includes grappling, joint manipulation, holds and controls on pressure points for submission holds *(pamislit)*. There are no holds barred, no limits on where and what to hit except in friendly workouts where injury to a workout partner is always avoided. You will quickly run out of sparring partners and friends.

Eskrima is an ancient fighting art, a product of a different culture and generation when guns and machine guns were rarely in use. With the coming of the cannon and gun power to the Philippines, Lapu-lapu and his brave warriors fell to the better armed Spaniards. The stick is anachronistic, archaic and obsolete as a weapon of modern warfare. Thus today, the art should be thought as a study of cultural tradition, both as a means of self-discipline, a means of exercise and as a means of fellowship with fellow eskrima enthusiasts. Through the art, we develop strength, balance, speed, reflex movement, grace and self-confidence but not as a fool hardy and stupid tool for aggression. This book is limited to the stick fighting aspect of the Filipino fighting arts. It is my area of expertise.

To appreciate Anciong Bacon's Balintawak Eskrima, you have to understand set-ups, anticipation, the art of outwitting through ruses and lures; economy and simplification of motion, sans lavish and squandered movements; effective strikes fused and bonded with speed, power, elegance and grace. That is the essence of Anciong's Balintawak and Anciong Bacon is the founder of this dynamic style.

The range of movements in eskrima in general conform to the natural movements of the human body. There are no extreme contortions, distortion, warping, deformation or abnormal twists of the human body to place extreme stress and trauma on ligaments, muscle and bone structure. The 12 strikes are normal movements that can be translated to other offensive moves in other martial arts. The stances are normal athletic stances, the steps are normal walking steps and the movements are typical and consistent with everyday human motions. With normal care and proper warm up exercises, the art can be practiced from a very young age to a very advanced age. As of this writing, I am 78 and one of my students is also in his early 70s and we still can do normal moves any young person can do. With experience and knowledge, we can pretty much spar with a young person, especially with a stick. Although eskrima is a complete martial art that includes weapons, bare hand combat and grappling, it does not claim the same intensity as mixed martial art combat used at the MMA tournaments. Although the real life battles are in fact worse—we master all foul blows and strikes, which includes, biting, eye gouging, knee and elbow breaks, grabbing or hitting the groin, submission holds, chokes and strikes to all knockout and hitting points and disabling strikes on vital parts using, fist, elbow, knee, head as well as knowledge and mastery of pressure points.

This book is written largely from personal experience and personal knowledge, as well as from oral history as told by the masters to the author and from other historical data elsewhere. I have set out to present the art from origin to modern times, as a fighting art, as cultural tradition and as a means of personal development. I hope you find it interesting, insightful and informative and that it inspires you to pursue Filipino martial arts in general, and Balintawak Eskrima in particular.

—Guro' Sam L. Buot, Sr.
Student, Teacher, Chronicler and
Balintawak Eskrima Historian and
Keeper of the Flame

PART 1

HISTORY AND MASTERS OF BALINTAWAK

CHAPTER I

A BRIEF HISTORY OF ESKRIMA

Map of Cebu from Google

Pre-historical speculation is that the early Filipino martial arts came with the wave of immigration of people of Malaysia and Indonesia bringing their own bladed weapons, probably in 200 BC. It is believed that later part in Philippine history some of those weapons may have come with Arab influences that also brought with them their religion in Southern Philippines in Sulu and Mindanao.

Discovery of the Philippines

In 1519 Ferdinand Magellan, a Portuguese unable to convince the King of Portugal, went and convinced King Charles V of Spain that if he sailed west, he could reach the Moluccas Islands, known for its spice, which would belong to Spanish Rule according to demarcations set in the Treaty of Tordesillas. On September 10, 1519, Ferdinand Magellan sailed southward across the Atlantic Ocean at the southern tip of America, now known as the Strait of Magellan, towards the Pacific Ocean. He had five ships – flagship Trinidad (110 tons, crew of 55 men) under Magellan's command, San Antonio (120 tons, crew of 60) commanded by Juan de Cartagena; Concepcion, (90 tons, crew of 45) commanded by Gaspar de Quesada; Santiago (75 tons, crew of 32) commanded by Juan Serrano and Victoria (85 tons, with a crew of 43, commanded by Luis Mendoza. The crew of 270 men included men from different nations including Portugal, Spain, Italy, Germany, Belgium, Greece, England and France. Antonio Pigafetta, a Venetian scholar, was appointed as chronicler to keep an accurate journal of Magellan's voyage—the first circumnavigation of the globe.

On March 6, 1521, they reached the Marianas Islands and Guam. Since the ships were robbed by the natives, he called the three islands Ladroni Island (Island of Thieves). On March 17, 1521, Magellan sighted the Island of Samar, marking their arrival in the Philippine Archipelago. On April 28th Ferdinand Magellan waded on the shores of Mactan and was met by Rajah Lapu-lapu and his men.

When Spain colonized the Philippines, eskrima was already the standard fighting art of the archipelago. Many authors and teachers institute fantastic stories of a "mother art" called "kali" in the Philippines that in reality was never found. They say Rajah Lapu-lapu, ruler of Mactan, was, according to Pigafetta, a kali expert. Well, the fact is, nowhere in Pigafetta's account is the word "kali" found. While we can only assume that since today the word Eskrima is prevalent in Cebu and Mactan, that that is the name of the art being practiced at that time. But what it really was, we do not know for sure. We only have a battle account and legend to inform us. In his book, *Filipino Martial Culture*, Mark V. Wiley quotes from Pigafetta's actual records, as follows:

> *"Our large pieces of artillery which were in the ships could not help us, because they were firing at too long a range, so that we continued to retreat for more than a good crossbow flight from the shore, still fighting, and in water up to our knees. And they followed us, hurling poisoned arrows four and six times; while, recognizing the captain, they turned toward him inasmuch as twice they hurled arrows very close to his head. But as a good captain and a knight he still stood fast with some others, fighting thus for more than an hour. And as he refused to retire further, an Indian threw a bamboo lance in his face, and the captain immediately killed him with his lance, leaving it in his body. Then, trying to lay his weapon on his sword, he could draw it out by halfway, because of a wound from a bamboo lance that he had in his arm. Which seeing, all those people threw themselves on him, and one of them with a large javelin thrust it into his leg, whereby he fell face downward. On this all at once rushed upon him with lances of iron and bamboo and with these javelins, so that they slew our mirror, our light, our comfort, and our true guide."*

This was the first recorded Filipino repulse of foreign invaders. When the Spaniards returned to overcome the Filipinos with their superior firepower and technology, sticks and blades lost. Eskrima became a prohibited art in 1596 and again in 1764. It was totally banned by Don Simon Aredo y Salazar since it was discovered that masters of the art led revolting Filipinos. It was also said that Filipinos were abandoning their farms to practice eskrima. Besides, the practice often led to injury and death. The art went underground and was taught by Filipinos—often from father to son.

It is believed that Eskrima crept into religious ceremonial dances *(sinawali)* and in Moro-Moro plays, depicting the conflict between Christians and pagans usually referring to the Muslims or Moros. It is said that sinawali dances concealed moves of offense and defense so that moves could not be forgotten. The Filipino national hero Jose Rizal, and other martyrs and patriots such as General Gregorio Del Pilar, Marcelo H. Del Pilar, Andres Bonifacio, Fr. Gregorio Aglipay, and Antonio Luna were practitioners of the art. Poet Laureate Francisco Baltazar (also known as Balagtas) made mention of Buno and Arnis in his immortal romance "Florante at Laura." The relevant part of the epic is also quoted in *Filipino Martial Culture*: "Larong buno't arnes na kinakitaan ng kanikaniyang liksi't karunungan" (The arts of Buno and Arnis displayed each one's skill and knowledge). Again, while some have re-written history to include the word kali in the work of Balagtas, we know it is not a fact.

It is said that eskrima was very popular with the Filipino Maharlika or royal blood. Although, it may have roots from other cultures, modern eskrima is Filipino, after WWII much of it truly Cebuano with other styles and versions from other provinces catching up to the trend. Post WWII, Cebu has been the epicenter of the eskrima cultural revolution. The common folk also practiced eskrima/arnis. In olden times, it was a game, sport, physical exercise and an art of self-defense. It probably started when early Filipinos discovered rattan (a long, tough vine, cut into convenient lengths), could be used as a good striking weapon.

Aside from sticks, bows and arrows, the early Filipinos were experts in bladed weapons. The bolo, pinute, kampilan or kris was a sidearm as the gun was to the West. This was especially true in Southern Philippines, which has influence from Indonesia, India, Thailand and Malaysia and more remotely from the Middle East from Muslim traders. The Muslims in Southern Philippines have a remarkable history of victories against foreign invaders, including the Spaniards,

Weapons of Philippines

Americans and Japanese. General John "Black Jack" Pershing's was still a captain when he was assigned in Mindanao to quell the Moro rebellion. The Moros were and are fierce warriors and the .45 caliber pistol was designed by Colt to stop the ferocious *juramentados*. The Muslim *juramentados* were suicide warriors and were unstoppable with lesser caliber weapons. Mindanao is rich in the variety of weaponry, since Muslim Philippines or Moroland used the bladed weapon as their deterrent against foreign invaders, not the least of which were the Spaniards, the Americans, the Japanese, their tribal enemies and lately the Philippine Army.

The Birth of Balintawak and The Eagle's Nest

The founder of Balintawak Eskrima, Venancio "Anciong" Bacon studied under the original known source of the Cebu eskrima knowledge, Lorenzo "Tatay Ensong" Saavedra, probably in the late 1930s in a style called Corto Linear. (Tatay is a term of endearment for father as in the American term "pops" or "dad"). Tatay Ensong organized what was then known

as the Labangon Fencing Club. He taught his talented nephew, Doring Saavedra, Momoy Cañete, and the especially talented Anciong Bacon. They were later joined by other Cañete brothers. Bacon and Doring were Tatay Ensong's most exceptional students. During the Second World War, Doring died at the hands of the Japanese *kempetai*. In 1952 the club was numerically dominated by the Cañete brothers. Bacon was frustrated with internal club struggles and politics and his further claim that the Doce Pares style was ineffective and seceded together with some of the better players of the club–among them labor leader

Anciong Bacon and Teofilo Velez

The King Eagle Anciong Bacon

Delfin Lopez and police officer Temoteo Maranga, and later joined by many more top fighters of the Doce Pares Club.

Anciong set up his clubhouse in 1952 in an obscure and modest downtown side street in Cebu City, named Balintawak Street. It was at the back of a small watch repair shop owned by Eduardo Baculi, a student of Anciong. This was located in the heart of downtown Cebu City, near the Corners of Colon and Balintawak Street. Balintawak is named after a historical placed called Balintawak in Caloocan, Rizal, where the patriot Andres Bonifacio made his famous cry for an armed struggle in revolt against Spain. This was later known as *Sigaw ng Pugadlawin* or "The Cry from the Eagles Nest" that eventually evolved into "The Cry of Balintawak." Historians say this event happened on August 19, 1896 and others say it occurred on August 23, 1896 and others say it happened on August 26, 1896. It seems that the official version is August 23rd, 1896 as declared by President Diosdado Macapagal. Regardless, it was Andres Bonifacio's Katipunero cry against the Spanish Guardia Civil in revolt against and displayed by the tearing of the cedulas. This was considered the start of the Philippine Revolution.

Thus, *Pugad Lawin* is symbolic of Balintawak and the Philippine Eagle. It is a metaphor of strength, independence, grace, beauty and majesty. The Philippine Eagle is the biggest strongest, tallest and one of the most magnificent birds in the world. It is the largest extant eagle specie with an average size of 91 centimeters long and 6.5 kilograms in weight and a two meter or 6.56 feet wingspan up to eight feet long. It is also known as the "monkey eating eagle" or *ibon'g hari* or king bird. It feeds on monkeys, small deer, pigs, dogs, pythons, chickens and even on other eagles in the air. It is only found in the Philippines and is an endangered species with only about 150 to 500 individual birds surviving. It is the national bird of the Philippines. The eagle's nest represents the lair from which Balintawak eskrimadors have left to roam, in fearless venture and to conquer the world. Anciong is our King Eagle.

The Golden Years of Eskrima

During the early 1950s with the emergence of Anciong Bacon and his Balintawak Eskrima, the art attained new heights. It is said that the Golden Years of Eskrima were in the 60s to the 70s heightened by the rivalry between Doce Pares and Balintawak. Even in Cebu, there were very few that identified themselves as eskrimadors. Filipinos were ashamed of their own art and never embraced it openly. Many Filipinos are colonial minded. They readily accept anything imported and were never proud of their own indigenous art. If you see pictures of even Doce Pares, they wore judo uniforms (*gi*) for workouts. Their exhibitions were

Balintawak and Doce Pares meeting with Johnny Chiuten, Momoy Cañete and Jose Villasin (seated), Teofilo Velez (squatting on the right), with Ben Marapao, Eddie dela Cruz, Max Tian and Bobby Taboada (standing).

mainly judo and jiu-jitsu exhibitions. Only in the last 30 years has eskrima caught the attention of world martial artists. There was a dearth of information about experts in the art. Since the 1980s eskrimadors have come out of the woodwork and inserted themselves in the limelight. By the turn of the 20th century "grandmasters" sprouted all over the globe asserting themselves as original experts in the art. Since the 1980s, eskrima has nosed its way to gain world attention and even some prominence. Early Balintawak eskrimadors were versed mostly in the Asian arts. Johnny Chiuten, Ben Marapao, the dela Rosa brothers Winnie and Romy, and Joe Go with his Tat Kun To school presumably taught karate, kung-fu and tai chi. All were convinced to learn Balintawak after trying and testing Anciong's legendary skills.

Eskrima Today

It was through the openness, sincerity and vision of Atty. Dionisio "Diony" Cañete that the Balintawak and the Doce Pares factions and other Cebu groups of eskrima started getting together and uniting eskrima as a Filipino fighting art. Cañete brought Cebu eskrima to national attention through Defense Secretary Gen. Fabian Ver. In 1975, Diony initiated the Cebu Eskrima Federation with meetings largely between the main rivals, the Doce Pares and the Balintawak Group and other smaller eskrima groups in Cebu including Larry Alcuizar's DIUREX, and Felimon Caburnay's La Punti Arnis de Abaniko. In those organizational meetings, Bacon, Villasin, Velez, Buot, Chiuten and Taboada represented the Balintawak groups. From the Cebu Eskrima Federation was born the NARAPHIL or the National Arnis Association of the Philippines, all through the initiative of Diony Cañete. Regardless, we

Sam Buot, Nick Elizar, Diony Cañete and Ike Sepulveda

cannot take away from the fact that GM Diony Cañete deserves the credit for bringing eskrima to national and international attention. In my visit to Cañete's studio in Cebu in September of 2013, Diony was very gracious and amiable. I give credit to Diony, Bobby Taboada and Nick Elizar for promoting amity, harmony and goodwill among eskrimadors worldwide, and now I am chiming in.

At the turn of the century, early eskrimadors came to the United States to work as migrant farmers, some coming via Hawaii to Mainland, mostly in California, bringing with them their native fighting arts which they even called estocada, again borrowed from the Spanish word meaning thrust as in the final thrust in killing of the bull. Many of these farmers were from Cebu, Panay, Samar, Batangas and the Ilocos region in Luzon and from Mindanao. There is little to no recorded history of the art. Most stories are circulated through tradition, legend and folklore. Many are apocryphal tales of their masters with healing and mystical powers, using *hilot* (massage) and *anting-anting* (amulets), which sounds too hokey and just hogwash for modern day practitioners. Some have pictures in Moro costume with bandanas and a kris for optics, to capitalize on the feared Muslim reputation. But the fact is, modern day eskrimadors wear baseball caps, tennis shoes and Nike workout pants, jeans or cut-off shorts, T-shirts and

probably karate gear at the dojo—gear which is not even Filipino. When we trained in Cebu, we wore street clothes to prepare for street confrontation with leather shoes to boot. I do train in normal workout gear, especially in the blistering heat of Phoenix.

Today, eskrima is a worldwide phenomenon. It has grown and propagated like wildfire, in the USA, Europe and Asia. The players are strong multi-faceted, equipped and train seriously like Olympic athletes. During olden times, poor fighters in the Philippines were tough and rag-tag fighter but mostly malnourished, ill-equipped and badly inadequate, deficient of any public or moral support. Polite society scoffed at them as bums, thugs, roughnecks or even criminally minded characters. It was not considered a sport or a thing of skill and pride with a drive for perfection. That is untrue in the world today, especially in the USA and now in Europe. Some of these new breed still need the technical skill and the deeper secrets of the art. Mostly from deep secrecy that have died with the masters. The seed has been planted and it is growing, developing and improving and with the seed of thought that is indigenous to the Philippines. One of the big promoters of Eskrima in the United States was Dan Inosanto, whose book, *The Filipino Martial Arts*, gave many in the Western world their first glimpse into these vast arts.

Dr. Mark Wiley

In the last 20 years, much of the grand exposure of the Filipino martial arts has come through the work of Dr. Mark Wiley. He was the first person to travel the islands and collect photos and interviews and video footage of the masters of all different styles. He documented this research in dozens of magazine articles and no less than a dozen books. He was never concerned with promoting himself, but with finding the true history, spirit, culture and masters of the Filipino arts and documenting them all for posterity. His books *Filipino Martial Culture, Filipino Fighting Arts, Arnis Reflections* and *Mastering Eskrima Disarms* (to name a few) have become classics in the field, offering insights into the history, culture, myths, masters and systems of over 70 different styles of eskrima and arnis. To my knowledge, his work was the first to state plainly that the so-called myth of the never-found "kali the mother art," was just that: a myth perpetuated by certain groups who used to call their arts arnis or eskrima. He received much backlash from those camps, especially in the USA, which is the only place the term was used at that time. But the older masters in the Philippines appreciated his work and respect him much. Without Dr. Wiley's efforts many of the older masters, now deceased, and their arts would remain unknown to the world. I am equally honored that he is the editor and publisher of this book, my life's work. Rey Galang should also be commended for his efforts to promote the Filipino arts, especially through his book, *Warrior Arts of the Philippines*, which features a photograph of Anciong Bacon on its cover.

Like many ideas that come to America, Americans make things better–sipa (known as "hacky sack") and the yoyo originated from the Philippines. It has been developed and improved beyond the imagination of their originators. The balisong and knife fighting, also an integral part of Filipino culture is a big thing among trained knife fighters. There are Filipino trained knife and stick fighters that have infiltrated martial arts studios and Hollywood. Hollywood has picked up Eskrima starting with American born Filipino martial artist extraordinaire, Dan Inosanto, with Bruce Lee in the movies "Enter the Dragon" and "Game of Death." More recently, "The Borne Identity" Series using dirty Filipino fighting techniques with Filipino fight coordinators, students of Dan Inosanto; also Dave Batista and Marrese Crump in "Wrong Side of Town" with eskrima fight sense, Denzel Washington in "The Book of Eli," James Bond of "Quantum of Solace," Tommy Lee Jones in "The Hunted" and "Death Drip" using the balisong and the "baddest" knife and fight scenes.

Pizza that came from Italy it is so much improved in the United States. I have tasted pizza in Italy and it is not anywhere near a Chicago style pizza and many Mom and Pop pizza parlors throughout the US. Even karate, kung-fu and tae kwon do from Asia are so developed in the US that natives of those native countries can no longer compete with Americans in those sports. The same is happening with eskrima. We have eagles that bred

Jose Villasin, Johnny Chiuten, Anciong Bacon and Teofilo Velez

VILLASIN-VELEZ BALINTAWAK WARRIORS L. to R. Fred Buot Jr., CNR, CNR, CNR, Tinong Ybanez (D), Nick Elizar, Ben Marapao, Winnie de la Rosa, Pilo Velez (D), Bobby Taboada, Johnny Chiuten (D), Bobby Tabimina, Jose Villasin (D), Hector Rizon (D), Sam Buot, Romeo de la Rosa (D), Nilo Servila (D), Chito Velez - Circa 1977 (CNR – Cannot remember, D - diseased) (Photo taken by Johnny Chiuten at Talisay)

in those humble nests and I was there where they bred. I have seen their lair and now they have spread their wings worldwide.

Fabled Masters and Challenges

The first Balintawak explorers were Teddy Buot, Remy Presas (student of Toto Moncal), Bobby Taboada, Nick Elizar and his sons, Monie Velez and this humble author (Sam Buot), who have taught starting in backyards, then in karate dojos and in complex training camps. Martial artists from the USA, Australia and Europe have imported our Filipino fighters to train them. So do not be ashamed of modest beginning and seemingly wild and improbable ideas. Now eskrimadors have come out of the woodwork with a plethora of self-anointed black belts and claims of being first. Of course there were Filipino migrant workers at the turn of the century that brought their crude native fighting art but they never brought the art to the forefront of public recognition. They were father to son traditions chockfull of superstition and anting-anting's which could never find currency in the real world of rough and tough fighters.

Youth and little knowledge are dangerous. Little knowledge is often taken as a license to abuse and misuse strength. Age, maturity and experience are often a cure for the "green belt" mentality. Aggressiveness and hostility often lead to undesired physical and legal consequences and may even lead to death. When I was young, I used to be gung-ho about the art and was eager to use my little knowledge in picking up confrontation. Age, experience and maturity tell me that knowledge of any self-defense is better if quietly and humbly possessed with coolness, composure and humility, not with arrogance and swagger. Once young, strong and quick, the best martial artists grow old too and develop arthritis and joint injury and pains. That is, if they are lucky enough to grow old, they will be a pathetic image of their former selves. They become mostly fat, gray, ashen, wrinkled, shriveled and sluggish—probably with shortness of breath and great joint pains. Also, I have seen the best martial artists and eskrimadors fall prey to untrained assassins.

Delfin Lopez, a Balintawak original, was a big, strong and brutal eskrimador. As president of the Allied Labor Union, he tried to pacify a strike at a rice warehouse. Unbeknownst to him a small, scrawny laborer assassin climbed on top of sacks of rice and jumped on him from behind, stabbing him above the clavicle with the knife going straight into his heart. He died on the spot with his mouth foaming and gurgling blood.

Eddie de la Cruz was a body builder, a nice fellow, Golden Gloves trainer and Balintawak eskrimador. Because he could not be confronted head-on, he was ambushed and killed. When you are known to be a martial artist, people in the Philippines do not confront you face-to-face. If they mean to kill, they will do so in an ambush. If you swagger, young guns will be eager to try you.

We have an eskrimador who is small and frail but possesses a frightful Charles Manson personality. He has killed three persons—one for what he thought was a lascivious look at his wife. Life in the old country was cheap and a person could literally get away with murder or be a victim of an assassination. Anciong Bacon himself killed a person in self-defense and was released from prison after a few years. We do not glorify his killing although it was done in self-defense. He was ambushed in the dark coconut groves of Labangon for the wrongdoings of his son.

The Truth of Bahad Challenge Matches

Many yarns and apocryphal stories about alleged grandmasters that have been in hundreds of death matches are purely myth. Duels are far in between. Like I said above, assassination is the way to get justice in these arts, not from a fair duel. Threats and challenges are often called off by the duelers. In formal fights, there are seconds and even written agreements. If no cooler heads intervene or if none cackles before the duel, then the duel (*bahad*) could occur. Mostly fights are ambushes with bolos or pinute, which often results in death or serious injury. There also have been verifiable cases where their Balintawak skills have saved them from attacks and possible death. Alleged death matches were just regular stick fights within the club and test of skills and sometimes from external challenges, none of which were serious enough. As for challenges, the better attitude is, Do not let your expertise get into you head! It is good to have skills and to know self-defense but it is no guarantee of survival. Avoid braggadocio you may get to live longer on this earth.

Trained martial artists are more circumspect with their knowledge and its deadly risks, let alone the legal consequences, of course. There are more bravado and bluster than real duels. In eskrima, there can be serious beatings that seldom results in death except when weapons such as guns, bolos and knives are used. There were of course gun battles and treacherous attacks which lead to death that have gained notoriety. They scarcely used skill, only deceit and treachery. Death mostly came with bladed weapons and in bygone times the use of hardwood bahi or kamagong in which a strike to the head had very serious consequences.

Even ultimate fighting, supposedly settling these disputes of the best fighting art, has really resulted in death matches. Teddy Buot told me how he stood as a second in a bahad issued by a fighter from Talisay, who challenged Anciong. According to Teddy, after a quick skirmish Anciong struck the man on the head and as he staggered, he quickly turned around, and rushed to pick up his buri satchel and ran off into the dark of the night. It was comical.

The Strength of Balintawak

Balintawak Eskrima does not claim to have all the answers and it doesn't. However, it does have moves and techniques that are unique to the art as well as moves similar to other fighting arts. A keen observer will notice moves similar to the art of Western boxing, and Chinese kung-fu in hand coordination, holds, trapping and more. It involves the use of the opponent's strength, as in Japanese judo, jujitsu and aikido. It includes bare hand combat as in shoot fighting, knife and bladed weapon defense, and disarming techniques as in combat judo. It involves grappling (dumog) and wrestling (layug) finger, wrist, elbow and knee locks as in jiu-jitsu. It involves choking and strangling (tu-ok or lo-ok). The art also involves kicking (pamatid or sikaran) as in karate Thai boxing and tae kwon do. However, little emphasis is placed on high and flashy kicks but rather stress is placed on short, snap kicks to the shin, inner and outer thigh, knee and groin area for direct, quick pain and effective injury. When the situation permits, round house kicks or swing kicks to the thighs and knees to the groin and body are applied. Sweeping, tripping and dynamics of balancing (*panumba*) are also a great part of the art. Mid-high frontal kicks have been used lately by students trained in other Asian kicking arts. It is used only if there is safety in delivery and not subject to dangerous counter-attacks. Recent survey shows that Filipino dirty fighting is one of the most effective fighting styles.

Balintawak Eskrima teaches counters to all forms of blows and attacks of all popular Asian fighting arts. It does not emphasize contortions or acrobatics, although stretching, warming up and cardiovascular conditioning, power strikes, power punches and delivery of blows plus muscle and strength development certainly make good sense. Recent students trained in other kicking arts have incorporated their art into eskrima. Many of our students have a wider training experience in multiple arts. Many of them are young, strong, and experienced martial artists—some have been or are in the police, military, law enforcement, athletes or just plain martial arts instructors with multiple areas of training. It would behoove me to acknowledge such fact and to humble myself for even be so audacious enough to teach them. They are humble and eager to learn something new, exotic and effective—a tribute to eskrima and the Balintawak style.

Balintawak Eskrima is not an ostentatious style. The deeper secrets of eskrima are hardly displayed nor will it be likely seen in print. Even if displayed, the moves are subtle, inconspicuous and innocuous that it will go unnoticed by even sophisticated and trained martial artists. Even hands-on teaching to trained martial artists requires repeated and detailed instruction and demonstration of the finer points of the moves. Demonstrations of the Balintawak style is sometimes dull, as Bach and Mozart are dull to unsophisticated musicians. That is the reason that some Balintawak seminars are laced, embellished and embroidered with flashy stick twirling by the young masters. Young masters have incorporated the *amara* (dance like moves) and Villasin's "Grouping Method" plus disarms to show more grace, sophistication and variety in its movements. The old school purists always thought that the showy "Hollywood-ized" and cinematic styles are ridiculous signature moves of rival clubs. The *amara* style is considered reminiscent of the 19th century flashy intimidation dances. Still a lot of techniques are locked and sealed until hands-on instructions finally thresh out the grain from the chaff.

All martial arts have their strengths and weaknesses. Very often, its strength becomes its weakness. The hard arts with power delivery of punches and kicks often lead to rigidity and inflexibility in changes of direction. In contrast, the fluid and softer arts may not have the same power of the hard arts. It is embarrassing to purists that some eskrima styles unabashedly copy other fighting arts and even use terms such as eskrido to denote the combination of eskrima and judo and eskribo to denote the combination of eskrima and boxing. These terms are unnecessary, since unrecorded history, fights progressed into holds, locks, grappling, wrestling, punching, kicking and throws when disarmed or unarmed. Undoubtedly, there is influence of other arts through infusion and osmosis by students with various backgrounds and training. Admittedly, it is a welcome part of growth. China built the Great Walls to keep the "barbarians" out. By shutting out the cultures of the world, it stagnated in its growth and development. It must be re-emphasized that eskrima is not a rehash, revision or imitation of other Asian arts. It is an art all its own.

Balintawak Eskrima, as with the rest of Filipino fighting arts, is meant to inflict serious injury and harm, using all means to inflict maximum harm. It is and it was the fighting art of the streets and the battle fields. It still is a survival tool. It therefore has hardly been promoted as a sport. In the mid to late 1970s, there was an attempt to "civilize" the art to make it safer and more acceptable to the parents of students and acceptable to sports promoters. By then, it lost some of its true essence as a self-defense martial art. In eskrima, strikes considered as foul blows in other sports, are taught, developed and mastered into a science. Strikes, thrusts with the stick, hands and feet to nerve centers and vital points are meant to cause serious injury—more obviously like strikes to the head, knee breaks, elbow breaks and thrust to the eyes, throat and groin hits or groin grab.

Transmission of the Art

Since its inception eskrima has been a very secretive art. It was often clandestinely taught from father to son or from a master to a trusted and loyal lifetime student. Until modern times, seldom were there large classes as it is predominant today in highly commercialized martial arts schools. It often takes years of detailed, hands on and individualized instructions. Some of the reasons for this are the detailed nuances of the moves as well as the intense club rivalries. Secrets

Jose Villasin instructing Sam Buot

of the techniques were kept so close to the chest. It took a lifetime before the deepest secrets were revealed by the master to his most loyal lifetime student. Absolute loyalty was the key.

To this day, Balintawak is still requires a one-on-one teaching method. That is, if you have to understand the nuances and fine shades of the art. Modern day schools have gone into lining up students and doing basic strikes. This cannot be a substitute for the personalized instruction of the master. This is commercialized teaching. Simple moves are broken down to obtain belts. This is ridiculous. I heard one school giving a white belt for learning strikes 1-6, the next belt for 6-12, etc. We never had belts. We were only as good as our last fight and you had to prove yourself every night at the clubhouse and did not get a pass for past glories and victories.

During club workouts, Bacon had several students and he had to make the rounds before he could spend valuable time with a student. Often, a student spent training time with his senior students by just the usual *palakat* with the head instructor or in sparring sessions with fellow students. Anciong would supervise instructions and executions were done correctly. When a student was waiting for an instructor, a student had to listen amid the din of clicking sticks, to what the Grandmaster was teaching other students. A diligent and attentive student could see, pick up and overhear valuable lessons. Therefore, although a student may have spent years at his club, he may not have spent that much time in personalized instructions from the Grandmaster. That is not to say that some of his assistant instructors were not proficient. They were excellent. Bacon's body was starting to deteriorate from a wasting disease. Many times, he took long time-outs through long lapses of conversation that would interrupt our workouts.

Oftentimes within the club, senior students did not share their secret moves and some teachers kept some secret techniques to themselves to keep the threat of a younger and stronger recalcitrant students under control. It was a form of insecurity in their abilities or a way of withholding secrets from a threatening upstart. This was to maintain dominance and control over a younger, stronger and talented student. Even with the most unselfish teacher, personal virtuosity is a perishable commodity that dies with the master when not taught and imparted or set to writing or recorded for posterity. That is the main reason for this attempt to preserve the style and secrets of Balintawak. So much, too much has been lost through secrecy. This feeble attempt is a frail effort to salvage and rescue the genius of Cebu's great Grandmaster Anciong Bacon and those who came after him.

Whatever is imparted here within the pages of this book is a superficial peek and glimpse into the reservoir of hidden and unrecorded knowledge and skills. Villasin taught me techniques which I refused to write down for fear it would be discovered. Like many hidden treasures, it has been lost and vanished forever. Much has been lost either because I did not grasp it, they did not teach it all or because I cannot remember it since I was foolish to hide it in my memory files where I can no longer find it. It may come as a surprise that different students of Anciong display techniques different from others taught at different locations and at different moments in time. Meaning, knowledge of one student may vary from the others, thus the need to compile and to share. We came from the same trunk but our branches look different

One of my ways of forcing techniques out of the grandmaster was by asking situational questions and "what ifs." Then, it would be amazing how he would unravel the conundrum with creative glimpses of genius. It is too late to wish for more time with the grandmaster. I wish I realized his singular importance at the time of my training. I never even bothered to pose for a souvenir picture with him nor did I bother to have pictures with the other masters and/or students—oblivious with witless ignorance of the significance that we were living in historical moments with soon to be fabled names in the pantheon of the masters.

Our martial arts schools then, were not similar to the school concept we have in the United States. It was more of a self-defense brotherhood—an exclusive club that met nightly and more extensively on weekends in the backyard of the master or the student. In the later years, it was a study in a controlled and cool-headed manner, attacks and counter attacks, the creation of situations and "what ifs." In Anciong's facilities, it was all workouts and no nonsense. At the Villasin-Velez facilities, sometimes, it became a social event accompanied by eating, drinking, and laughter, storytelling and teasing.

The young ones bragged about their recent scraps as the master either acquiesced or cautioned them about the responsibility that accompanies strength and knowledge. The master talked of the incongruous topics of self-control and being level headed while teaching the refined secrets of the deadly art of combat fighting. Testy and cocky troublemakers were quickly put in place by being rapped on the knuckles, humiliated, blackballed, snubbed or even ejected from the club. If a student wanted to advance in the art, it was best not to be a threat to the junior instructors or the master. It was best to take the position of a student—humble, meek and eager to learn. Respect for elders and the master, to this day, are written on a stone tablet. To the chagrin of their students, I know of one who regularly brags of beating Grandmaster Bacon and all named masters. He keeps on talking about it now that the Grandmaster and other masters are dead. This obviously is tall tale. He may have accidentally hit his teacher, who was there to teach and not to show his superiority. To this day, he is a pariah and worse of all, he

Anciong Bacon teaching Jose Go

Anciong Bacon teaching Jose Go

is considered a nut head. To the mortification of the more knowledgeable, he gets a pass from an uninformed worldwide crowd.

The day a student asserts his superiority over a senior is the day he must be able to defend his art in the arena. If he wins, he would get higher in the pecking order and would have earned his place, sadly, like the animals in the wild. The "greenbelt mentality" of arrogance and bravado is shunned. Quiet confidence and maturity command respect. In relating an incident requiring the use of force, the force had to be justified by non-aggression and the necessity for self-defense. Seldom was the club visited by outsiders, foreigners, and students of other arts or members of rival clubs. Any presence was treated as a case of flagrant espionage or a challenge to the club. This often resulted in serious challenges and fights. A volunteer fighter increased his standing among his peers. The tale of the fight was embroidered, garnished and exaggerated as it was passed from mouth to mouth, depending on which side was telling the story.

During the early era when the art was new, control was less prevalent. There were senior practitioners who were mean and malicious; brassy beginners often suffered brutal pain before learning, which also lead to vindictive students and harsh teachers. Even Anciong would inflict some pain, if only to emphasize a point. After repeated emphasis, a student would be warned and if a point was not learned, a rap could follow and the lesson would be quickly learned. Lately, there has been an effort to encourage rather than discourage beginners. Villasin was an advocate of gentleness and ease with beginners so do most of the new masters.

Capt. Octavius "Jimboy" Hife tells an Anciong anecdote when Delfin Lopez would beat up the other students. Crudely translated, Anciong cautioned Delfin, "Chuy, if you keep on doing what you are doing, I will not be able to earn a living." Meaning he would lose his students. Anciong said, "Well, let's you and me play." In a few skirmishes, Anciong dumped Delfin to the corner of the workout area threatening to strike. In embarrassment, Delfin said, again loosely translated, "If you were not Anciong, I would have shot and killed you." Delfin was a scary and violent man.

Bacon did not personally succeed in promoting his art beyond Cebu since he lacked education, self-promotion, showmanship, and theatrics to promote his art. He was not prone to grandstanding and flamboyance in the promotion of his art. He was unable to communicate, write or preserve his art for posterity. His students have picked up his standard banner and carried on his battle. To my chagrin, many ill-equipped, even incompetent, yet more audacious proponents of the art have reaped more attention and publicity in martial arts magazines.

For many years, there was a very strong rivalry between clubs. There were no club visitations, sharing or display of techniques. Everything was held close to the chest. There was always a running battle of bad-mouthing the other clubs and styles. There was also a deliberate attempt to suppress Balintawak as a style. It has been called the Cebuano style, the rival club or other names except Balintawak. The name of Anciong Bacon was studiously avoided and omitted. Together with the propaganda were claimed championships of contests and tournaments. As a member of the Board of Directors of the Cebu Eskrima Federation, I was present in the meetings arranging the supposed tournament. The Balintawak masters boycotted the contests when rival clubs jockeyed to set the rules, chose the judges and pair the contestants. Among others, Balintawak mocked the idea of wearing armor for protection. Balintawak wanted unarmored full contact. In the end, this has caused snickers and ridicule among Balintawak eskrimadors with the foregone "crowning ceremonies."

Lately, on the internet, the Balintawak brand can no longer be contained. Too many spurious clubs claim affiliation and even training under Anciong, Velez, and Villasin. Consider this, these masters died 25 years ago or longer. Anyone less than 40 years of age was a suckling, uncircumcised (a rite of passage for boys in the Philippines) and in his shorts. Anciong died in 1980, Villasin died in 1988 and Velez died in 1989. Anyway, Balintawak has spread like wild fire. Balintawak and Anciong Bacon are now very much a central part of the history of eskrima and arnis. Since many of its moves have been openly taught to hundreds and published in many publications, the signature moves of Anciong Bacon are now part of the eskrima lexicon. Words like *tapi-tapi* (checking hand), were meant to be words of ridicule and derision are now used by rivals and taught as part of their own curriculum. Since Bacon used the tapi or slap down of a checking hand, the mockers caricatured it and called it *tapi-tapi*. That's how the term was born. Words like *tukwas, paawas,* and *sablig* are now part of the eskrima lexicon. The Philippines is the new face of the martial arts world and the unsung heroes are the old masters that mostly died poor, penniless and unheralded. I am doing my share in telling the story of both the departed and aging and battered warriors.

CHAPTER 2
THE MASTERS OF BALINTAWAK

"Grandmaster"—so few deserve the title.

In eskrima, there is no official body awarding the title of Grandmaster. As far as I am concerned, there is and will always be only one Grandmaster of Balintawak, and that is "Anciong" Bacon. There are younger master that have risen in the ranks. I can think of a few, as teachers, innovators, and promoters of the art. It is crucial that they know they can teach and that

L to R: Chito Velez, Romeo de la Rosa, Nene Gaabucayan, Anciong Bacon, Rey de la Victoria, Bobby Taboada and Teofilo Velez (Photo by Johnny Chiuten at Fort San Pedro, 1976)

they have made an impact on the promotion of the art. Many sophomoric eskrimadors have claimed the title "grandmaster" or even a heady title of "supreme grandmaster" in a trivial manner, as if attaining a self-anointed black belt. The term has been trifled and cheapened—it has become worthless. Who grants these grandiose and spurious titles of grandmaster anyway? Is it just bald-faced egotism and immodesty?

Historically, none of Anciong's students or contemporaries dared call themselves "grandmaster." Lately, names like Bobby Taboada, Nick Elizar, Chito Velez, Dr. Ben Marapao, Capt. Octavius "Jimboy" Hife and Nene Gaabucayan come to mind as possessing skills required of the title. Yet some of the new breeds of so called "grandmasters" have neither seen nor studied under Anciong. What's more, some of these 30-some "grandmasters" were still unborn when the masters trod this earth 35 years ago; and those born were still suckling. Who elevated them into that vaunted status? As far as I am concerned, bestowing upon you such a title is plain delusion of grandeur, more accurately called megalomania. After Anciong, a precious few have risen anywhere close to the title.

As one of the most senior surviving members of this team, I propose that for a teacher to carry the title of "grandmaster" they must be appointed as members of the Balintawak Grandmasters Council. Others may have the skill but have had little-to-no impact in the promotion of the art, and so should not hold the title. I proposed to Bobby Taboada and some elders of Balintawak, that only a Board of Elders who preferably directly studied under Bacon and/ or Villasin, or those with credentials of competence and knowledge of the art, be granted the title of Grandmaster. That on top of his training and competence in the art he must have contributed towards the promotion, study, teaching and innovation of the art but never by self-acclaim. All current "grandmasters" are virtually self-proclaimed and self-anointed, although I personally would want to reaffirm the title to these deserving intrepid warriors and pioneers of the art. As I earlier said, there is no official body granting such titles.

As one of the oldest, if not *the* oldest, surviving student of Anciong, Villasin, Velez, and Teddy Buot, some of my contemporaries have attributed to me the flattering title of Grandmaster. That is not for me to bestow upon myself. I just call myself *guro'*, the accepted Tagalog or Filipino word for teacher. Sometimes the Spanish word *maestro* is used in Cebu. Purists, however, called teachers *tig-agak* or tutor, from the root word *agak*, which mean to teach. My students call me *manong* (elder) or *kuya* (older brother). That suffices for our cultural respect. It is a stunning thought that Anciong died in 1980, and both Velez and Villasin died by 1989, and that I am now the old man of the art. There are few direct students of Bacon that are left that can tell the story. For sure, none I know have recorded it, few can tell it, much less write about it for posterity from personal experience and involvement. The responsibility I feel is overwhelming.

As can be seen among the Balintawak warriors that I have highlighted below, they truly were and are warriors and fighters for survival. Independently, they have sailed the world, conquered the odds of extreme poverty and made a name for themselves and for Balintawak. Among the fighters mentioned in the previous chapter, they have developed their skills; they have blazed the way, giving honor to both themselves and their masters as true fighters, warriors and conquerors. Even some of their daughters have departed from the shores of want to overcome and sail to new horizons. That is the indomitable Balintawak fighting spirit—a warrior's spirit of survival. Below, I would like to give acknowledgment to the grandmasters of Balintawak, beginning, of course, with the art's founder and first Grandmaster, Anciong Bacon.

Grandmaster Venancio "Anciong" Bacon
The Diminutive Genius of the Art
Ibon'g Hari — the "King Bird"

Grandmaster Venancio "Anciong" Bacon was born October 15, 1912 in Carcar, Cebu, Philippines and died on November 1, 1980. He was married to Catalina Decatoria Bacon and had lived in Labangon, Cebu City with his four children. Benedicta was born 5/20/43, Meliton (birthdate unknown.) "Leonie" was a petty thief who was murdered, Carina was born 11/15/50, and Amparo was born 5/04/53. Anciong was small man, no taller than 5'2" and less than 120 pounds soaking wet. In 1952, several other skilled eskrimadors such as Delfin Lopez, a labor leader, fearless fighter and police officer, then Lieutenant Timoteo "Timor" Maranga (later, Major Maranga), joined by Jesus Cui, Isidro Bardillas, Lorenzo Gonzales and Andres Olaibar defected from the Doce Pares group when Anciong Bacon organized the Balintawak Club. It was called Balintawak because the clubhouse was located on Balintawak Street behind watch repair shop owned by Anciong's student Eduardo Baculi, with no realization or aforethought of its historical significance.

Delfin Lopez was known to be big, tough and a sadist at times. He was nice to those he liked and was a pain to those he disliked. He was probably 5'10" to 5'11" and 180 pounds or more. As a teenager, I was even afraid to have eye contact with him. Lt. Timor Maranga was a member of the Cebu Police Force, had his own unique style which was quietly ridiculed in the club but in retrospect, these were practical, dangerous and effective fighting moves, which are now currency. For his time, he was also a big man for a Filipino—probably 5'9" to 5'10" and about 180 to 190 pounds. What I remember about his moves, was the *cabra* to the groin and up to the throat and other creative thrusts. Although, I never trained with him at the club since I tended to stick to Anciong. I did not even train with Arturo Sanchez or Jimboy Hife, since they were assistants training beginners and other students. This was after Teddy Buot left for the US in 1973.

Anciong Bacon, the King Eagle

Anciong Bacon and Teddy Buot

In class we waited and paired off with those we felt comfortable training with, as Anciong would do the rounds to *agak* or tutor individual students and move on to the next. There was always a feeling of distrust of being smacked on the knuckles by a sadist instructor, eager to hurt a beginner. At this time I was already a lawyer, commuting between the Villasin-Velez Group on Mabini Street in the Parian District and Villasin's homes in Lahug and his home on Legaspi Street near Plaza Independencia, and Anciong's club—wherever it was. Anciong had his club at various locations: the Aboitiz Building on Borromeo Street, the Enad Building on Juan Luna Street, the Go Chan Building on Magallanes Street, and later at the home of Roman Encarnacion in Labangon. I followed him wherever he held sessions.

Jesus Cui, Ationg Abella, Lorenzo Gonzales, Vicente Olaibar, Isidro Bardillas, Inting Atillo, Eduardo Baculi and Jugo Milan were all there before my time. I could not attach a name to the faces of these people in the club. I did not know them. I did see Eduardo Baculi, but I never knew him personally. He seemed always to be hunched over the watches in his watch shop with that monocle magnifier over his eye. Vicente Atillo had his own Mambaling style that was similar to Delfin Lopez and Jody Lopez. They joined Anciong, as Anciong innovated and revolutionized the art. Atillo was followed in his art by his son, Crispulo "Esing" Atillo. They practiced the Mambaling style used by Esing's father, which Esing earlier called the New Arnis Confederation and later called the Philippine Arnis Confederation. With the rising popularity of Balintawak, he has now latched on and christened his style the World Balintawak Arnis-Eskrima Association. At the time of the birth of Balintawak, Esing would have been in his

Aciong Backon and Jimboy Hife in headlock

early teens. At the time I joined Teddy Buot at the Balintawak Club in the early 60s, I was in my early 20s. I did not see any young men or teenagers. Teddy was probably the youngest of the group in his mid-to-late 20s. Contrary to tales, there were no children or teenagers at the Balintawak site. They were all tough, grizzled and battle scarred fighters.

Anciong advocated direct, economical and effective moves. Nothing was wasteful, fancy or ornamental in his moves; nevertheless, they were graceful, elegant and most of all, efficient and effective. The other stylists brought their own basic training methods, styles and specialized talents and these were picked up and learned by the young masters by osmosis. Their techniques were tested at workouts and, thus, the evolution of the art. Oftentimes, they were specialists in certain fields of combat, such as knife fighting, boxing, wrestling or they were just brawlers. There was unspoken internal rivalry and each kept his own specialty as a secret weapon in club workouts. They were eventually picked up, analyzed, copied and integrated by all in what is now under the banner of the Balintawak style.

Anciong was not only innovative and original, he was fearless. The reason Delfin Lopez and Timor Maranga, both big men, joined Bacon was because both men tested their skills on Bacon and in both instances, Bacon humbled them. Bacon was the proponent of the *kwentada* method, often claimed by many but seldom understood. Part of his training was as a wrestler and boxer. Anciong's theory was to master the single stick because it was a more realistic scenario to have one weapon rather than multiple weapons when attacked. He used the free left hand for boxing, pushing, pulling, shoving, parrying, clearing, checking, monitoring distracting, and manipulating the opponent's stick, hands and body. He also developed the checking hand in what is now known as *tapi-tapi* (to parry or fend off) as the rebuking or scolding (*badlong*) hand. It was used in lieu of the *daga* or dagger that was used in earlier training and earlier styles. This was at first ridiculed by his detractors, since double sticks was the standard of the day. Originally, the term *tapi-tapi* was used as a mockery or jeering ridicule for the move, the way the term protestants was used to mock those who protested against the Catholic Church.

Today, it is imitated and openly studied by rival clubs, eager to know Anciong's secret of success. The legend is that Tatay Ensong took the short stick or *daga* from Anciong when he would stab his sparring partners. Whether that is a fable or fictional, the truth is beside the point. Anciong created, innovated and mastered the single stick and stuck to its practical usage.

For practical purposes, fighters seldom have the luxury of having a weapon and much less two weapons on hand. Today, the single stick is widely imitated and copied by rival clubs, who in the past advocated that two sticks were better than one. Anciong abhorred the fancy stick twirling, a signature of the "rival club," as being impractical in real fights. Another apocryphal story is that he did not know how to do the *amara*. This sounds preposterous since there is no mystery in the method. Bacon's moves were music in motion: direct, graceful, balanced, effective and powerful–even mysterious and baffling.

Anciong Bacon and wife, Catalina

Anciong was master of the mind game or psychological warfare. Anciong preached and practiced what he called, "taking the power" away from your opponent, or the mastery of his opponent's mind. That was quite prodigious for an unschooled man to speak of psychological warfare and mind games.

Bacon's grave site marker

Anciong was a genius of his art, certainly an audacious claim, not by Anciong but by his pupil. He was fabled and legendary—loved and respected by his students, hated and feared by his rivals and lifetime enemies, but never disrespected. He was the single most deadly living practitioner of the art during his existence with verifiable battles (*bahad*, or full contact duels) to his name, including one that landed him in jail for homicide. He killed a man, an enemy of his son, who waylaid him in the dark among the coconut trees in Labangon. His lawyer failed to convince the judge that what he did was done in self-defense. His lawyer apparently failed to prove that he used necessary deadly force to defend his life. Until his death in 1980 at age 68, this little man humiliated young, strong and disrespectful *karateka*, martial artists and eskrimadors, often landing them on the seat of their pants with him standing over them in a menacing manner. His talent was esteemed, admired and even romanticized and embellished by his students and admirers. He was also shunned or avoided by his rivals. Other fables have since cropped up on the internet claiming hundreds of death matches by Anciong. This is wholly untrue, pure fiction. Regardless, he was a prodigy and master of his art that gained the respect and admiration of both friend and foe. He died very poor, just like Van Gogh and Mozart, the great composers and artists of old. He had no clue of the veneration that followed him after his death.

Jose V. Villasin
Lawyer, Labor Leader, Teacher and Friend

Jose V. Villasin (Nov. 5, 1923 to Nov. 5, 1988) was a lawyer and labor leader. He and his wife Juliana had 14 children, only five of whom were boys, four of whom are still surviving: Ver (Boy), Joey, Bianor (Banoh') and John. As a lawyer and officer of the Allied Labor Union, laborers respected his intellectual skills but dockhands also understood power, might and physical supremacy. As a teacher, he never intentionally hurt his students. He tried not to inflict unnecessary hurt and resentment on the part of students since it produced cruel next generation teachers. Villasin was the first to dissect the works of Bacon in an academic and written fashion. He taught eskrima and martial arts at the University of the Visayas. He tried to organize his course by making mimeographed notes for his students to organize the thought process of the grandmaster by dissecting and breaking down the art into understandable and digestible morsels for beginners. It was an outline with sketchy descriptions of moves. Incorporating it in demonstrations varied the demonstrations to make it more exciting, appealing and less monotonous.

It was under the personalized tutelage of Joe Villasin that the author had a quick start and understanding of the basics, intermediate and advanced studies of eskrima. Villasin's study simplified and organized the moves for a quicker understanding and the development of reflexive reaction to strikes from all directions. Purists dismiss his attempt as a corruption of the Grandmaster's thoughts and methods. During demonstrations, the unchoreographed moves were varied and more exciting—instead of the dull and repetitive strikes during *palakat* or *seguidas*. The ultimate strikes were controlled even as they appeared real. They used these fight choreographies for their *moro-moro* scenes during fiestas and movies. Villasin's work was the first attempt to reduce Bacon's art into writing. I doubt that any of it has survived. This *palakat* pattern later evolved into the Grouping Method that further enhanced the patterns into a more varied and wider-range diversity of strikes.

Villasin was a great teacher—soft-spoken, gentle and always with a ready smile. It was wrong to underestimate his portly and rotund stature. If he heard or noted a blowhard talking about his toughness and adventures, he would lead him on and allow them to really hang himself. He would then lead him and say, "Oh, that's great! Go on, tell me more." He would ask him, in a sheepish and innocent way, "So how did you do it?" The braggart would continue to lengthen his hang rope by speaking out of turn. For the final *coup de grace* (French for "blow of mercy") he would say, "Show me." That was when Villasin would show him his total ignorance of self-defense and especially of eskrima. Villasin was strong as a bull but graceful and agile in his moves as incongruously displayed in his tango and cha-cha dance moves. It was wrong to misjudge his self-deprecating humor and easy smile. Beneath his humility was great confidence and conviction of his ability in his art.

Jose Villasin's legacy is kept alive by his son Ver and other sons in the Philippines, Bianor, John and Joey, and certainly by this grateful author. Unfortunately for these younger Villasins, their skills never saw the light since their light has been "hidden in a bushel" in the corners of Cebu, unexposed to international drumbeat and hoopla.

Villasin at Fraternity induction

Jose Villasin was president of the Balintawak International Self-Defense Club and this writer was his one-time vice-president when he was still in the Philippines. At the time the club was called "international," it was more in playful humor since there was nothing of any international flavor. Only Teddy Buot was in the United States. Even then, Teddy did not particularly ally himself with Villasin and Velez who, presumably, he took to be heretics. The use of the word "international," however, has proven to be a self-fulfilling prophecy. Balintawak has since gone international with Bobby Taboada traveling worldwide holding seminars and organizing Balintawak clubs over the entire world, Teddy Buot doing his teaching in the east coast and Sam Buot doing his little part in the Phoenix, area. Other eskrimadors like Bobby Tabimina, Nene Gaabucayan, Ver Villasin, Monie Velez and Nick Elizar have since picked up some slack. Their students and successor of their knowledge have also spread worldwide.

Villasin later moved classes from Legaspi Street to his home in Lahug. This author helped him acquire his home as a reward for removing squatters from the lot of Atty. Eddie Gabriel on Salinas Drive in Lahug. The Grandmaster, Anciong Bacon, often came to visit and do check-ups on the progress of his students or just to visit and socialize. He may originally have been threatened by the opening of eskrima clubs which were in competition with his school, but he eventually came to accept the fact that these were his "children," loyal students, heir of his knowledge and defenders of Balintawak—especially during the organization of the Cebu Arnis Federation (which included all eskrima clubs in Cebu). Anciong Bacon, Jose Villasin, Teofilo Velez, Sam Buot, Johnny Chiuten, Bobby Taboada and Chito Velez represented Balintawak. Meetings were tense, paranoid and suspicious as to intent and motives. There always seemed a potential for erupting into explosive violence. Jose Villasin's name is now spread worldwide with many bogus claims of tutelage by the master. He is survived in his art by his

Sam and Villasin atop SSS building

sons and daughters teaching and propagating Balintawak Eskrima, more particularly by his son Ver in California.

Teofilo "Pilo" Velez
Teacher, Faithful Soldier, Organizer, Host and Promoter

Teofilo Velez (Dec. 17, 1918 to Feb. 17, 1989). Unknown to most, the home of this humble man spawned some of the greatest fighters of Balintawak. It was the cradle of many Balintawak fighters. The young men were dauntless and fearless fighters that swung live blades in jaw-dropping, death defying exhibition matches with fearless abandon. That same boldness translated into sailing the winds like eagles to conquer the world of martial arts. His home was the nest that spawned some of the most prolific students and teachers of Balintawak warriors worldwide: Bobby Taboada, Nick Elizar, Winnie and Romy de la Rose, Nene Gaabucayan, Ben Marapao, Bobby Tabimina, Chito, Eddie and Monie Velez, Eddie de la Cruz, Nilo Servila, the Villasin brothers and myself. With these few, many have learned; with these

Teofilo Velez

few, many have heard; and with this few, Balintawak Eskrima is a worldwide phenomenon. Unfortunately, some have died before their time to blossom.

Few people have promoted the early Balintawak art as Teofilo Velez did. He housed the club at his home where nightly workouts of the Villasin-Velez branch of the Balintawak club with check-ups by Grandmaster Bacon. His senior instructors were Bobby Taboada and his sons Chito and Eddie Velez. Bobby was a more dedicated student of the master. Bobby was often used as "dummy" during demonstrations. To show realism, Bobby often suffered cuts on the forehead with strikes. It was brutal! In one event, Bobby wanted to show off his skills. To cool

Balintawak International Villasin, Velez Group picture with Chito, Bobby, Ben, Villasin, Velez, Johnny and Eddie squatting

off his up and coming student, Velez (who was a natural lefty and thus ambidextrous) shifted his stick to his left and gave Bobby a big whack which served as an object lesson on humility to his young upstart. Demonstrations by Bobby, Winnie, Romy, Ben, Chito and Eddie were realistic and very scary fighting scenes—using real knives unrestricted by precautionary measures, with split second thrusts and parries, with little or no safety precautions. These were men of great skill sets, many of them just not

Monie Velez

having the opportunities to display their wares on the international market.

After college in the early 60s, with my practice of law and business, martial arts fell in the back burner for me in matters of urgency. It was through Velez' repeated invitation that I resumed eskrima studies. The visit to his club started to become nightly and my interest intensified. Villasin also came nightly for workouts at Velez' backyard on Sikatuna Street at the Parian District until Villasin resumed his classes in his own backyard, also on Legaspi Street. Velez' backyard was a few square feet, with a kitchen and laundry on the side and benches around to accommodate the seated students. We were always sparring at very close quarters, literally and figuratively.

Velez was a friendly and affable fellow, quick to grab your hand and shake it uncomfortably long before releasing it. He was a loyal soldier and a faithful defender of the Balintawak name. He was also a good teacher. In his humble means, he often hosted get-togethers at his home for the Balintawak members. He was a recruiter for and promoter of the art. At his home, he ruled with an iron fist, taming his three sons, his daughter and Bobby Taboada. He was also a graceful dancer as he and Villasin would sneak out to the dance school to the consternation of their wives, early evenings to learn cha-cha and tango steps. Their wives held tight reins on them but that did not dissuade them from slipping out to learn the dance steps. Their dance grace interpreted into graceful eskrima moves and style, characteristic and distinctive of Balintawak Eskrima.

Teofilo Velez

The Balintawak family owes Velez gratitude for the multitude of students that were loyal to the style because of his own loyalty to Anciong and to Villasin. Velez was the PR man of Balintawak—amiable with friends but fierce in the defense of Balintawak, especially severe and stern and uncompromising in handling his boys and Bobby. Unforeseen and unpredicted by Anciong, Velez and Villasin, the few they taught are teaching and spreading their art worldwide.

The Velez boys, Monie, Chito and Eddie

Teodoro "Teddy" Abellana Buot
A purist of Bacon teachings, often "reclusive, withdrawn and inaccessible"

Teddy Buot

Teddy Buot was the oldest son of Ricaredo A. Buot and Remedios Abellana. He was born on July 1, 1931, at Cebu City and died July 4, 2013. Although trained as both a mechanical and electrical engineer, he too was fascinated by the deep sophistication of Anciong Bacon's art of eskrima. He, in great probability, has spent more time in eskrima than in engineering. The proud and strong man was relegated and banished into his wheelchair and eventually died seven years later from the stroke he suffered in 2006. When he was healthy, aside from eskrima, he kept himself fit playing basketball with young Filipinos until his devastating stroke.

Teddy studied under Anciong Bacon starting in 1959 and was his head instructor until his departure for the United States in 1974. I know the old man Anciong had a tender spot in his heart for Teddy. Out of respect for the Grandmaster, Teddy did not call himself Grandmaster; and neither have Villasin, Velez and Anciong's original students. His students called him "Manong Ted" (Manong is a Cebuano term of respect used for an older brother). Teddy lived with his wife, the former Dennie Sanchez in Southfield, Michigan. After his emigration to the US in 1974, Ted's brother-in-law Arturo Sanchez took over as head instructor of Bacon's school. Sanchez came to the US and returned to the Philippines where he eventually passed away. Ted was like an older brother to me and I followed in his footsteps in the art of eskrima. We both were fascinated by the high bars, both lifted homemade weights from concrete molded in clay pots and both graduated from the foul-smelling boxing gloves that were available in the deprived Labangon neighborhood.

Dan Inosanto & Ted Buot, 1995

Teddy Buot, Erwin Ballarta and Michael Lohmier

Anciong and Teddy, pre-departure

Ted & Students with Anciong

Anciong, Teddy with weekend Balintawak training

Ted and Anciong workout at Ted's backyard in Katipunana Street, Cebu City

Ted and I were next door neighbors and that's where I learned my eskrima rudiments. I remember Ted riding his Harley motorcycle in a slow, confident and proud rumble down Katipunan Street. Family disagreements (which none of the kids want to remember), age difference, studies outside the province of Cebu for me, and Teddy's eventual move to the US, kept us apart—even being in the US kept us apart. Ted lived in Michigan while I lived in the greater Phoenix area. Eskrima proved to be the bond bringing both families together. If there was anyone who could claim himself as heir to Anciong's style, Teddy could rightfully claim himself as the standard-bearer of the purist Balintawak style eskrima. He disapproved of any teaching different from Anciong's teaching, thus he dismissed Villasin's "grouping method" as non-original, apocryphal and a departure from Bacon's teachings. With near certainty, he was the longest personally trained survivor of Anciong Bacon until his demise. Unfortunately, for the art, Teddy, like Anciong, was not a mass media hog to promote his name and the art. One of his students will have to carry Anciong's

Teddy and Jimboy Hife, circa 1960

Teddy and Irvin Ocanada

Teddy Buot and Erwin Ballarta   *Teddy Buot and Jimboy Hife*   *Teddy Buot and Remy Presas*

flag for Teddy. He was described as "reclusive, withdrawn, and inaccessible" and accepted only personal students—strictly by recommendation.

Bobby Taboada
Multiple awards recipient and prime promoter and advocate of Balintawak Eskrima worldwide

Bobby's Taboada

Guillermo "Bobby" Taboada was born in Cebu City, Philippines, on November 6, 1948, the oldest of five children of Sergio and Gabriela Taboada. He grew up fighting in the streets of Cebu, (not because he was a troublemaker but because it was the only means of surviving those streets). He is soft spoken and very slow to anger except when he rises in defense of himself, and luckily that is infrequent and almost nil.

He was first introduced to eskrima by his father. He also boxed for six years and went into the exotic and imported arts of karate and kung-fu. Bobby left home when he was 12 and later lived with Teofilo Velez as an "adopted" son and student of eskrima. That literally meant sitting at the foot of the master in full obedience and loyalty in his search for knowledge and wisdom. He then learned the secrets of Balintawak Eskrima from Jose Villasin and Anciong Bacon. Bobby discovered that the art was deadly, effective and sophisticated. As a fearless and undaunted volunteer for fights and tournaments, Bobby was trained by all the Balintawak masters in the practical aspects of combat fighting. In this light, it must be emphasized that in the Philippines, eskrima is not a sport in the traditional sense of the word and therefore not governed by safety rules—especially in earlier times. It meant combat fighting and sometimes fights to the finish (*bahad*). Only lately have there been efforts to make it safe as a sport. Bobby is a long way from the street battles in Cebu, where he has experienced violent and deadly fights,

Bobby Taboada

some with multiple opponents. He has also witnessed full contact duels. As a security guard for Bisaya Land Transportation and Bisaya Shipping Lines, he figured in real combat—fighting scavengers, who tore sacks of rice at the pier to steal rice. He fought multiple opponents of over 10, some armed with knives and sticks, out to attack him. Armed with only an eskrima stick, he positioned himself with his back towards the sea to avoid being surrounded. The rest is history — this is a story that Bobby does not even want repeated.

Bobby eventually broke the bonds of poverty after meeting a New Zealander, Peter Ball, who took him to New Zealand, starting out miserably, not knowing the language, culture and perennially broke. He lived in New Zealand for 12 years and almost a year in Australia. In the early 90s, Bobby came with Ball, Paul Ballagoie and his family to the US with hopes of immigration. In 1991, I heard from my student about an eskrima seminar in Phoenix supposedly held by a Balintawak eskrimador named Bobby Taboada from Cebu. I went to check it out and to my great surprise and delight, it

Bobby demonstrating during a fiesta

Bobby Taboda, Greg Sepuveda, Sam Buot, Ryan Buot, Ike Sepulveda, Craig Smith and Irwin Carmichael

Las Vegas candle lighting ceremony (03-11-08) - Sam Buot, Jorge Penafiel, Bobby Taboada, Bobby Tabimina, Nene Gaabucayan

was in fact my stable mate! Bobby was attempting to seek permanent residence in the United States. There was a fraternal bond between us due to our common training under Velez and Villasin. Bobby and Peter Ball's family lived in my townhouse for about a year as I helped them settle.

Fallout with his partner Peter Ball, eventually lead Bobby to relocate North Carolina. There, he established new alliances with Irwin Carmichael who he met in Australia at a martial arts seminar. Bobby has since resumed his extensive seminars in various parts of the United States and worldwide. He has an extensive network of clubs established worldwide—from Europe, Australia, New Zealand and the Americas. He has travelled worldwide doing seminars and demonstrations to gasping, gaping and wide-eyed audiences.

Bobby currently lives in Charlotte, North Carolina, where he has established his World Balintawak Headquarters. He is now on a mission to promote Balintawak worldwide. His primary emphasis is on defense techniques, which he has continuously researched, tested, re-tested, innovated and improved. He teaches law enforcement officers, martial arts instructors, black belts and advanced students from all styles of martial arts, who he thinks have attained the maturity, discipline and capacity to absorb the skills and techniques. In his 45 years of experience in martial arts, he contends that the hardest thing to learn is how to defend. The easiest thing to learn is how to strike, hit, punch or kick. That is why the techniques he teaches places primary emphasis on defense. Bobby is also an innovator, probably a departure from the traditional Balintawak methods. He has developed drills, exercises and innovative techniques uniquely his own. That however is the fundamental nature of growth. He is a good teacher with a delightful sense of humor and flair and style all his own. Don't ever give him the karaoke microphone. He loves to sing and does a credible job at it too. His daughter in New Zealand is a professional singer in the national limelight.

Bobby Taboada has made several videos for commercial worldwide distribution. He has incorporated original and innovative exercises and drills and even fancy stick twirling, *amara*. This has been assailed and criticized by purists as a desecration and a defiled version of the Grandmaster's art. They are however, eye catching and they do sell tapes and seminars. Today, Bobby Taboada is the most visible advocate of the Balintawak style of eskrima, leaving everyone in the dust. Bobby is a long way from the oppressive slums of Cebu City. He is more polished and has eradicated some of his old crude ways. He does not allow vulgarity and swearing during training. It is one of the reasons he will flunk his students during exams—either by swearing or dropping the stick through disarm. Now back in health after a near fatal illness and surgery in 2011, Bobby is back on the saddle clearly slimmer and just as agile and strong. He is a success and the consummate example of the achieved and accomplished American

Bobby, Craig, Sam 11-12-2010

Bobby Taboada, Bart Vermilya, Craig Smith and Sam 11-10

dream. His life would make a great action movie but unfortunately can be credibly acted by only Bobby himself.

Samuel "Sam" L. Buot, Sr.
Historian, chronicler, author, student and teacher

Samuel L. Buot, Sr., was born in Cebu City on March 24, 1936, the eldest son of Alfredo and Susana Lagrito-Buot. He grew up in the rough neighborhood of Katipunan Street in the Labangon District of Cebu City. He was first exposed to eskrima by his cousin Teddy Buot, who lived next door. Sam left home at the tender age of twelve to study at Silliman University in Dumaguete, Negros Oriental, from high school through law school. Eskrima training for him at this time was limited to the summer vacations. Except for some neighborhood boxing, with smelly gloves and old-fashioned bare-knuckle brawls, serious studies of the arts did not occur until after college in the late 1950s and early 60s. Besides education, the university polished his dull edges with some culture in a Christian University established by early American missionary Horace B. Silliman which later became Silliman University. Despite smoothing of the rough edges, the

Sam Buot 11-24-2011

enduring Darwinian theory of "survival of the fittest and elimination of the unfit" never left him. You can take the boy of out the asphalt jungle but can never take the asphalt jungle out of

Las Vegas - Sam Buot, Jorge Penafiel, Topher Ricketts, Myrlino Hufana, Bobby Tabimina, Bobby Taboada, Nene Gaabucayan, Raffy Pambuan, Scott Samuel (3-11-08)

Steven K. Dowd, Sam Buot, Bobby Taboada, Jorge Penafiel, Nene Gaabucayan, and CNR

Bobby Taboada, Bobby Tabimina and Sam Buot

Sam Buot, Jorge Penafiel and Nene Gaabucayan

the boy. After college, Sam found himself heir to his father's struggling real estate business. He developed subdivisions, acquired real estate and had probably the most successful brokerage firm in Cebu City at that time period building his career until he eventually became national president of the Philippine Association of Realtors Boards.

After college, Sam resumed his eskrima studies, although business and his law practice competed for his time. During martial law in the Philippines in 1972, owning firearms was a capital offense, punishable by death. The only legitimate way to defend one-self was through martial arts. This intensified Sam's interest in the martial arts, most especially eskrima. Self-defense

Sam 11-25-14

Sam Buot, Peter Hill, Wally Jay, Willie Lim, Peter Ball, Kathy Golden and Rico, circa 1991

became an urgent matter for self-preservation. He was smitten by the sophistication, finesse and elegance of the art, especially since it was indigenous to the Philippines. In the age of colonial mentality, nothing home grown was deemed good, only foreign made goods and imported ideas were believed worthy. It dawned on Buot that the Philippines had something original and native, which was comparable and arguably even better than many concepts of self-defense. As a staunch nationalist, he wanted to promote the Filipino art. This time he could afford to hire the best instructors. He proceeded to hire all talents in eskrima and other martial arts—including Anciong Bacon. He worked out during and after office hours until near curfew hours at midnight and more intensively and extensively on weekends. This went on until Martial Law triggered his departure for the United States. Eskrima obsessed him. It was a way to escape his frustration with the oppressive, dispiriting and kleptocratic Martial Law regime of the conjugal dictators Ferdinand and Imelda Marcos.

This book is an expansion of Sam's notes on eskrima started when he was under the tutelage of Atty. Jose Villasin. Sam had his own dark room and took pictures with Villasin to capture the subtleties of the moves. It was an attempt to record and organize the voluminous material dished out every day in workouts. Immigration to the US in 1978 aborted the effort but the idea never left the author. Serendipitously, with the collapse of the real estate industry in the late 1980s, the author found time to regroup, focus and intensify his efforts in finishing the book. Publication fell again into dormancy with the constant addition of notes, never seeming satisfied. With constant demand from internet readers of his site, he played with the idea of placing them on PDF CD's in harmony

Sam demonstrating at Filam

The soaring eagles – Masters Nick Thompson, Ryan Benjamin Buot, Sam Buot, Adam Tompkins, Bart Vermilya and Craig Roland Smth)

Balintawak Demonstration Team (10-24-10)

Sam, visiting GM Willie Lim and Ryan

with more current technology. In 2013 Dr. Mark Wiley, an eskrima master, publisher and historian, approached Sam about reorganizing his work into the book you read here.

Timoteo "Timor" Maranga Sr.
Rough, tough and all-around athlete and police officer

Maj. Timoteo Maranga

Timor Maranga was one of the original secessionists from Doce Pares together with Anciong Bacon and Delfin Lopez. He had his own style, called Tres Personas Eskrima de Combate (aka: Combate Eskrima Maranga) founded in 1968. Timor ruled the tough district of Pasil in Cebu City. At his time, Pasil was the toughest district in Cebu City. Manong Timor was an all-around athlete. He excelled in swimming, shot-put, discuss throwing, boxing, wrestling, jiu-jitsu and eskrima. His motto was *Hitupngan pero dili hilabwan*, meaning, "Equaled but never surpassed."

Timor was battle tested in WWII in league with Leo Giron and Antonio Ilustrisimo, and was a member of the famed "bolo battalion." His instructors include Emilio Tadio, Faustino Tanio, Rogelio Ortiz, Imo' Sagarino, and Dalmacio Salinguhay with mixed styles. He grew up in Oango Island, Sta. Rosa, and east of Mactan Island, in the mainland of Cebu. He met with Eslao Romo an eskrimador of the tough Pasil area by the wharf of Cebu and the founding fathers of Doce Pares, Doring Saavedra, Lorenzo "Ensong" Saavedra, and Anciong Bacon, founder of Balintawak, where both later seceded from Doce Pares Club.

Timoteo "Timor" Maranga was an officer of the police department. He always showed up at Anciong's studio but I never worked out with him since I did not know him well enough. He had a unique style which he called Tres Personas de Combate, apparently named after the Holy Trinity. Many ridiculed his style but in its way were very effective and difficult to counter. I particularly remember his *cabra*, a ripping stroke from the groin up. He had thrusts from behind. It seemed funny but it was really very unique. He was contemporaneous with Anciong in seceding from the Labangon Fencing Cub.

Timor died in June 1988. He has left his legacy to his son Rodrigo "Drigo" Maranga, a proud heir to his father's art and who is doing an outstanding job in promoting it. Drigo promotes his father's art not only in Cebu but in Europe as well.

Nick Elizar
"Little Anciong" — A new star of Balintawak is born

Nick Elizar has brought Balintawak beyond his native Cebu City and has traveled worldwide holding seminars and spending months, mostly in Europe where he has been holding seminars and organizing clubs. Nick Elizar is another self-made man from Samboan, Cebu. He trained with Jose Villasin and Teofilo Velez together with Bobby Taboada, Sam Buot, Nene Gaabucayan, Ben Marapao, the dela Rosa Brothers, Velez brothers and the Villasin brothers.

Nick was born in September 1948 in Ronda Cebu. At five years old, his family moved to Cebu City. It was here where he met Bobby Taboada, a childhood friend. Both their families worked for Don Vicente Gullas as caretakers of the Gullas' farms. Gullas was the founder and owner of the Visayan Institute, now the University of the Visayas. It was here that Nick eventually went into eskrima, serendipitously with his friend Bobby Taboada under the tutelage of Teofilo Velez and Jose Villasin. He also dabbled with boxing, popularized then in the 1960s by Cebuano fighting legend Gabriel "Flash" Elorde. He also ventured into other Asian fighting arts of karate and tae kwon do. He eventually found his home in eskrima after he trained with Villasin and Velez in 1972. The club was visited and checked by Anciong Bacon during which Anciong would check on all students.

Nick branched out to Dumaguete City when he discovered Ricardo Abellana who had previously trained with Villasin. When he returned to Cebu City, he organized his own club in Banawa; in the meantime he drove a taxi for additional income. As a taxi driver, he encountered a life threatening hold-up where he successfully used his eskrima skills to subdue his two passenger

Nick Elizar and Sam at Nick's Cebu Headquarters

assailants. He has had multiple fighting skirmishes over which he has convincingly acquitted himself.

In a formal ceremony in Lapulapu City in 1982, Teofilo Velez awarded 12 of his most advanced students the title of Master, Nick was one of them. The new club was named the TeoVel Balintawak Group, named after Teofilo Velez. Nick has worked as a body guard to prominent businessmen and worked as a member of the Cebu City Civil Security Unit. Today he works at the office of the Cebu City Mayor's monitoring group. In 2003, Nick organized his club known as Nickelstick with two chapters in Banawa and on Don Pedro Cui. He conducts weekly training at the Ayala Park. Today, Nick travels abroad, organizing branches of his World Nickelstick Eskrima.

"Mighty Mite" Nick is now 65, not much larger or taller than Anciong, still strong, wiry and quick. He is still youthful both in looks and movement and has attained maturity and wisdom as a martial artist and as a person. He trains students who come from all over the world to his club in Cebu City. He is considered one of the best products of the Villasin-Velez branch of the Anciong Bacon legacy. His is still an on-going story with his sons Ned and Neal quickly picking up the pace. Like Bobby Taboada, Nick has had the daring, entrepreneurship and sense of adventure to conquer the world. I searched out Nick in my last visit to Cebu in September 2013 where we had a chance to fellowship with the Sepulveda brothers, Butch and Ike. We even visited with erstwhile rival Doce Pares GM Diony Cañete, who was as amiable and affable as could be expected.

Balintawak get-together at Nickelstick Headquarters (8-16 2007)

Nonato "Nene" Gaabucayan
Alumnus of the Villasin-Velez block of *Balintawak*

Nonato "Nene" Gaabucayan of Cagayan de Oro and Los Angeles was among the fabled and daring Balintawak warriors, together with Bobby Taboada, Chito and Eddie Velez, Nilo Servilla, Nick Elizar, Ben Marapao and the de la Rosa brothers Winnie and Romy. At 16 he was a boarder of Ben Marapao where he learned about eskrima. At 18 he had his own students in Lapulapu dividing his time between his studies at the Philippine Aeronautical School and the Lapulapu YMCA. After his studies in Cebu he returned to Cagayan de Oro and organized the TeoVel Chapter of Balintawak. Like the intrepid Balintawak eagles, he has soared and spread his wings

Nene Gaabucayan

to Australia, Switzerland, and Germany where he stayed in Europe for three years. He is now settled in California.

In November of 2008, during Bobby's shindig in Henderson, Nevada, after 35 years in Balintawak, Nene was conferred the title of Grandmaster by Balintawak Elders Grandmasters Bobby Taboada, Sam Buot, Bobby Tabimina and Jorge Penafiel, in acknowledgement of his contribution to the art. To my knowledge, he is the only one who was conferred the title by his peers. He earned it. In that Nevada meeting, he took it as an opportunity to display his special skills with his stick, more especially the breaking of coconuts with a single flick with his stick. The people were all in awe and amazement. It was a spectacular display of skill, speed and power.

Octavius "Jimboy" Hife
747 airline pilot and long-time student and assistant to Anciong Bacon

Jimboy Hife 6-03-2014

Jimboy Hife is the nephew of Teddy Buot and Arturo Sanchez, as good an eskrimador as any and yet unheralded and unpublished since he was mostly in the skies. He kept his credentials by teaching wherever he was stationed, mostly to his fellow pilots, his crew or whoever took interest. He, together with Arturo "Turo" Sanchez, took over the assistant instructor responsibilities when Teddy Buot left for the US. He is one whose talent in the art was suppressed and obscured because of his other professional and more financially rewarding skills and profession as an airline pilot.

Arturo Sanchez, Jimboy Hife, and Anciong's daughters – Carino, Amparo and Benedicta (2009)

Jimboy, Anciong and Taby Lim

When flying, he never failed to check up on the old man and to go and visit his family and help with their needs. When Anciong died, he had the bones of Anciong and his wife Lina exhumed and reburied in a decent grave beside the chapel of the San Nicolas Cemetery chapel with a grave marker for all those who may wish to visit. If you visit Cebu, it is near the San Nicolas Cemetery Chapel.

To the author's fading memory, the original students of the later generation of Bacon at his club included Arturo Sanchez, Teddy Buot's brother-in-law, Dr. Abraham Zerna, and Jody Lopez, Capt. Octavius "Jimboy" Hife, Bobby Tabimina, Roman Encarnacion, karateka and *Tat Kun To* school owner Joe Go, Dr. Cres Go and this author. Later, I met Tinong Ybanez socially but at that time he had already suffered a stroke, so he was no longer at his prime. The worldwide Balintawak Family owes Capt. Octavius "Jimboy" Hife for his unfettered loyalty. Jimboy has been a source of anecdotes about Anciong and his eskrima.

Johnny Chiuten
A special case and an exceptional and outstanding talent

Johnny Chiuten was a kung-fu, tai chi and eskrima master. He was originally a fierce *Balintawak* enthusiast but out of frustration with the secretiveness of the Balintawak masters, suspicious of his kung-fu and tai chi style, he joined Felimon Caburnay of the Lapunti (Labangon,

Punta Princesa and Tisa) Eskrima Club. Johnny gave me private instructions in kung-fu which I found too strenuous and demanding. Johnny Chiuten was probably one of the highest ranked kung-fu practitioners in the Philippines and was president of the Philippine Karate Association. He took some of the historical photos of Balintawak during his early association with Balintawak. Johnny together with Villasin, Velez, Buot and Taboada represented Balintawak Club during the organizational meeting of the Cebu Eskrima Federation led by Doce Pares Young Turk Atty. Dionisio "Diony" Cañete. Diony and I passed the law bar exams the same year. Diony was the son of my dear friend Rufino "Pining" Cañete, who frequented my father's office as a real estate agent.

Johnny Chiuten

Bob Silver "Bobby" Tabimina

One of the original warriors of the Villasin-Velez Camp of Balintawak

Bob Silver "Bobby" Tabimina was originally from Iligan and now has his camp in Pasig, Rizal, but travels worldwide doing Balintawak seminars in Singapore, Great Britain and the United States. He came to know of Balintawak in 1967, when his father, Col. Olympio N. Tabimina, then Deputy Chief of Police of Iligan, asked around in Cebu for the best martial art instructors and subsequently learned that there were only two worth learning: Doce Pares and Balintawak. The Colonel however was advised to steer clear of Balintawak, as they were considered reckless and wild due to their tough and painful training regimen. Knowing that Bobby would only be interested in a true fighting art, Col. Tabimina chose Balintawak and with the help of his contacts, subsequently made arrangements for Bobby to train with Atty. Jose Villasin, one of Anciong's more well-known instructors.

Being a karate black belt and experienced fighter by then, Bobby was skeptical about Balintawak, thinking his background would enable him to hold his own. Atty. Jose Villasin was familiar with this skepticism however, and knew what was needed to cure this attitude. On their first meeting, Atty. Villasin asked Bobby to attack him, in any manner he knew how. Afraid at first that he might accidentally hurt Villasin, Bobby attacked only probingly. Each attack was effortlessly countered. Embarrassed and frustrated, Bobby decided to attack in earnest but in every case Villasin thwarted his attacks and showed Bobby how vulnerable he was to counters. Humbled and convinced, Bobby decided then that he had to learn Balintawak and began to train with Atty. Villasin.

Las Vegas - BobbyTaboada, Bobby Tabimina & Sam Buot

After training for six months under Atty. Villasin, Bobby was endorsed by Villasin to Teofilo Velez for the continuation of his training. Like Villasin, Velez taught Balintawak using the grouping system. However, Bobby was given special training as he was being trained as a fighter. It was during this period that Bobby learned Teofilo Velez's Balintawak, well known for its fast, tough and hard-hitting approach. It is said that Tatay Velez's brand of Balintawak was more suited to those who wished to become true fighters. Bobby trained and fought for Tatay Velez for four to five years, and credits much of his teaching philosophy of "sharing everything you know" to Velez.

In 1971, Tatay Velez told Bobby that "he had nothing more to give" and declared it was high time for Bobby to see the "old man" (Anciong) and learn from the founder himself. At the time, however, Anciong was incarcerated in Crame for killing a man who ambushed him—Anciong's justification that it was self-defense was rejected by the courts because he was an acknowledged Balintawak master and should have exercised more restraint. But that's another story.

Undeterred, Bobby traveled to Manila to seek out Anciong. With the help of his father's contacts, particularly Col. Nadorra, C1 of Camp Crame, Bobby was able to arrange a meeting with Anciong. At this first meeting, Bobby wasted no time and unabashedly told the founder the purpose of his visit and requested Anciong to test him. The founder accommodated his request in his inimitable manner. With broomstick handles as improvised weapons and only the jail guards, his father and the Provost Marshall as audience, Bobby and Anciong proceeded to "play."

Bobby in no time learned why Anciong was Balintawak's grandmaster. Despite his over five years of experience and training by this time, his attacks and defense were still nowhere near the level needed to overcome Anciong and he found himself on the receiving end of Anciong's painful stick, punches, kicks and trips. Shocked but challenged, Bobby soon became Anciong's regular and only visitor, taking care of his needs. In return for this genuine concern and kindness, Anciong trained Bobby further, refining and modifying his skills. Anciong later revealed to Bobby that his Balintawak had evolved and is the reason Bobby had a difficult time coping.

When Anciong was paroled, he flew not to Cebu, but to Iligan City, where he continued to train Bobby one-on-one. In the months that followed, Anciong continued to spend most of his time in Iligan training Bobby, occasionally going to Cebu only to satisfy his parole conditions, a fact known only to a handful of people. It was during this time that Bobby learned, and became proficient in, the updated version of Anciong's Balintawak.

Pacito "Chito" Velez
Eldest son and designated heir by his talented brothers

As the oldest brother, Chito Velez has been designated by his brothers as the heir apparent to their father's legacy. They have reorganized themselves and call their organization WOTBAG (World Original Teovel's Balintawak Arnis Group). They teach at their Guadalupe site and at the Ayala Park. The brothers concentrate their teaching on flexibility, timing, speed, hitting points, defense and knife fighting. This is a system they learned from their late father which he in turn learned from the late GM Anciong Bacon. WOTBAG has started to reach worldwide with seminars in Germany and Poland with youngest brother Ramon "Monie" in the lead. Monie is the seeming spokesman of the clan and the "Michael" of the family. Eddie, although the second child is actually the "Sonny" in this family, a violent kid with a scary temper and frightening scorecard. I will not elaborate.

Chito Velez

Mark Wiley, Chito Velez, Abner Pasa at the Velez home, Cebu City 1999

The Velez Boys are all outstanding eskrimadors. Chito has always been a volunteer fighter and so was Eddie—known for their bold and daring real knife demonstrations with a seeming disdain and contempt for life. Monie was still a very young pup when I was with the club, so I have not seen as much of his play. From the looks of it, Monie is just as outstanding an eskrimador as his big brothers. The youngest of them, Monie is showing the daring of conquest as a soldier of fortune that has sent him to Europe and to scale the walls of success. Some eskrimadors in Cebu are just trapped and held down in the glass ceiling of poverty and absence of opportunity. Part of the cause of the many young eskrimadors falling behind in their search for recognition is the seeming insurmountable odds of breaking loose from the chains of poverty. Out of dampened spirits, many have fallen to despondency and alcoholism.

Evincio "Ben" Marapao
An optometrist by profession and a bold, rough and tough eskrimador by avocation

Ben Marapao, one of the original Balintawak Warriors

Ben Marapao, an optometrist by profession, was one of the original Villasin-Velez Balintawak warriors. He is a 5th Dan black belt in Okinawan karate. He is a dedicated Balintawak Arnis/karate combatant with devotion to the Villasin and Velez banner of Balintawak. He calls his system the KGB MAGGS (Kritter's Group Marapao Aggression System). Still largely centered in Cebu, his realistic combat fighting is gaining worldwide acceptance.

Ben started martial arts in the 1960s in Kodukan judo and thereafter became a karate instructor at the YMCA. He later concentrated on Balintawak Eskrima after joining The Villasin-Velez branch of Balintawak. He is a contemporary of Bobby Taboada, Nick Elizar, Dr. Abraham Zerna, Sam Buot, Winnie and Romy dela Rosa, Chito Velez and later joined by younger brothers, Eddie and Monie Velez.

Ben's style teaches full contact reality fighting using Balintawak style dirty-fighting methods and techniques as the foundation of his art. He is a natural lefty. He is a firm believer in power, speed and aggression. His style may soon find greater acceptance as a new Balintawak approach to the Anciong legacy. Ben is one of the talented, daring and fearless fighters of the old Balintawak School. Unfortunately for the world, being an optometrist has kept his skills locked within the borders of Cebu where he balances his profession, family, business and eskrima. Ben is shadowed in his art by his talented and motivated son Junjun Marapao.

Ver "Boy" Villasin
Sometimes an outsider because of his travels and yet the most passionate follower of his father

Ver "Boy" Villasin was born on August 15, 1953 in Cebu City. Friends and family refer to him as "Boy" Villasin. Son of Atty. Joe Villasin, Ver is a proud standard bearer of the Villasin banner. When I was working out with the boys, he was on ship as an adventurous and thrill-seeking sailor. As a boy, he would watch his father teach lessons to his friends and students from a window. He wasn't allowed to watch until he turned eight years old since his father thought he would misuse what he learned to beat-up his school mates. Temper control was among his first lessons in Balintawak Eskrima. Balintawak Eskrima reminds him of his time with his father. Boy started learning the art at the age of eight and like any normal child, he was playful and was crazy about all the games children played; but his father was persistent in teaching and after the lessons and practice, he would of course run down to join his friends. Like most children of masters, the kids do not really appreciate what they have. When the young master reached his teen years, was when he started getting serious with eskrima. By then, he became one of his father's instructors in the "old Balintawak School."

Ver Villasin – Torch bearer of his late father Atty. Joe Vilasin

In 1970, his father asked him to form a new club for the Villasin clan and called it Balintawak Arnis Academy. Ver Villasin was appointed by his father as the president, Jingga being the vice-president, Ethel was the secretary, and the younger brothers John, Joey, and Bianor were among the Board of Directors and other officers. As a father, Atty. Jose Villasin dreamed having one of his children follow his footsteps as a lawyer. He asked Ver to come home and study law. Conceding to his father's wish, he came back to Cebu in the 80s to enroll in San Carlos University. Being a member of a large family, Ver worked for Philippine Airlines in order to support his education. He concentrated on his studies to satisfy his father's desire. Finally in 1986, he graduated with a major in Business Law.

Several years after his graduation, Ver retired from Philippine Airlines as an Operation Manager and returned to Australia before coming to the United States. Once in California he started the Villasin Balintawak Arnis Academy/Balintawak International, now currently in the North Bay Area. He trains his students on Tuesdays, Thursdays and Saturdays. Balintawak Arnis Academy is often invited in different city events to perform and demonstrate the art. All this he did, to continue the legacy of his father Atty. Jose Villasin and "Tatay Anciong" Bacon. Ver like Bobby Taboada and Nick Elizar refused to be captive to the tyranny and subjugation of poverty of his native country. Even as a young man he joined the merchant marines to see the world.

Like all the intrepid young men of Balintawak, in 1972 Ver traveled to Italy, the Netherlands, Brazil, Greece and Australia. This was where the rest of his family and other relatives resided. Anywhere he traveled to he taught Balintawak Arnis although he did not stay long enough to establish roots. He has eventually settled in the USA where he has his home and has raised his family. Pare Joe would be proud to see his children Ver, Vivian, Cheryl, Techie, Ethyl, John, Bianor and Joey—am I missing any?—all spread worldwide.

Notes on Other Masters of Balintawak

There are now many spurious and unverifiable claims of training and tutelage under Anciong Bacon. They cannot be verified by Bacon since he has been long dead. Even his students have gradually passed on. The history of Balintawak Eskrima is gathered mostly from oral history. There is scant information or first-person accounts. Most have been through oral history told by the remaining few who were personal witnesses to history. Many search for the truth and some color their stories to promote their own biases and agenda. To the author's great sadness and dismay, almost all of the great original Balintawak eskrimadors have since died over 30 years ago. Venancio Bacon, Jose Villasin, Teofilo Velez, Timoteo Maranga, Jesus Cui, Delfin Lopez, Tinong Ybanez, Isidro Bardilas, Arnulfo Moncal, Ationg Abella, Lorenzo Gonzales, Hugo Milan, Eduardo Baculi, Vicente Atillo, Teddy Buot, Arturo Sanchez have all passed. The few remaining originals are Octavius "Jimboy" Hife and Sam Buot, and a precious unknown few. Many of them are forgotten or personally unknown to the author within his

Anciong Bacon and Joe Go

Anciong Bacon and Joe Go

own period of training and of course many have since passed away. Their skills, talent and genius have also perished and died with them. It is incumbent upon the living to reconstruct, collect and preserve the wealth and science of the art for posterity. It has been my personal burden.

Not all of Anciong's students appeared at the club regularly nor did they appear at the same time. They came to different locations and at different moments of the Grandmaster's life. If I saw them, many were unknown to me and I had limited contact with these original people. It was very seldom that Teddy brought me with him. I was still a student and was mostly in school at the neighboring province of Negros, except for summers and I was very timid in joining the big boys except as an observer. Besides, I really did not see any teens or young men among those battled scarred fighters. Instead, I had my scant training with Cousin Teddy at Uncle Ricar's backyard. Even then, Teddy gave more training to Tony Abella, Jimboy Hife, Ludy Ocanada and Jody Lopez.

I have met Delfin Lopez and I recall meeting him at Times Kitchen on Juan Luna Street. He carried a side arm and a baton from the tail of the stingray (*ikog sa pagi*), with a woven leather strap. With his sidearm, he sat at the corner of the restaurant with a very distrustful and guarded look scanning the people in the room. People never made eye contact as this could be considered suspicious, challenging or even an act of aggression. Felimon Caburnay also had his own style. He and Delfin Lopez were part of the original Labangon Club and later seceded in the early 1950s to form what was soon to be the Balintawak Club. During workout sessions, I met with Jimboy Hife and Arturo "Turo" Sanchez, brother in law of Teddy Buot. I also never worked out with either of them since I preferred to train with Anciong. They were his teaching assistants at his club.

Dr. Cres Go

I know of important people including politicians who may not want to be mentioned in this account. One is a friend of mine, a Philippine Senator. The late Mandawe Mayor Pedong Ouano was not shy about being known as a Balintawak eskrimador. Some rich Chinese men were private students of Anciong, including the late Dr. Cres Go. He and Joe Go, a *karateka* and Tat Kun To school owner, were private students of Anciong. Pacifico Pelaez, a world renowned guitarist, studied with the Villasin-Velez group.

I met with Dr. Cres Go during one of my visits to Cebu while doing my own research on Balintawak and its remaining practitioners. Dr. Go has made faithful and devoted international friends and students, among them Hilmar Siebert of Lorach, Germany. In the United States, to the author's knowledge, only a handful living eskrimadors can claim to personal instructions from Anciong Bacon. Many more came at various times in these masters' lifetime and career. No offense and disrespect is meant for the omission of many.

Dr. Go at Cebu Hills

There were other talented and unsung and unrecognized students of Velez and Villasin. I have sparred with all these men. They were all brave, daring and tough. There were other younger students who I did not know, neither did I work out nor associate with them. My association with the young guns ended when I left for the United States in 1978. Some of these students were before my time. The success and/or failure of these young men of eskrima are the story of struggle and survival in a perennially impoverished country. Some equate their toughness with alcoholism, hooliganism and misguided machismo. Others have truly searched to better themselves with ambition and drive to escape endemic and oppressive poverty. Others have just been kept down by a "glass ceiling" of deprivation, desperation and hopelessness. Some

Dr. Cres Go

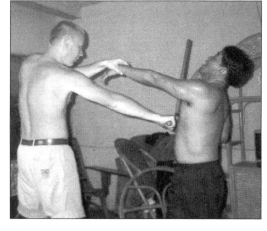

Hilmar Siebert and Cres Go   *Hilmar Siebert and Cres Go*

just passed away before they had the opportunity to bloom. For many, old age has just caught up with them which have toned down their machismo and ambition.

There were other eskrimadors which in a way were associated with Balintawak. As told by Teddy Buot, others practiced the old Mambaling style, Vicente Atillo, whose style was the same as Delfin Lopez', the original group that seceded from Doce Pares, together younger guys like Jody Lopez and Vicente Atillo's son, Esing Atillo, a student of his father Vicente Atillo in Mambaling. Esing called his group the National Arnis Confederation, not a part of the Balintawak group. He has recently identified himself as the World Balintawak Federation, obviously aligning himself under the Balintawak banner and calling himself a Balintawak "original." When Balintawak was organized in 1952, Esing was at most 14 years old. Just the facts. I am older than Esing and in 1952 I was 16 and graduated from high school. He also claimed to study under Doring Saavedra who died during WWII, meaning Esing was a toddler of three or four years old when this supposed study happened. Jody Lopez and Delfin Lopez always allied themselves with Balintawak. Other well-known eskrimadors like Remy Presas had his Presas Ilongo style, and was a student of Arnulfo "Toto" Moncal, who was a student of Timor Maranga, an associate of Anciong. Presas was already world known for his book on Modern Arnis and his moniker as the "Father of Modern Arnis." He became an enthusiast of Balintawak style after a visit by Villasin at his Manila studio and eventually became a friend of Teddy Buot and Bobby Taboada when he was in the US. As a historical fact, I do credit Remy for his promotion of arnis/eskrima as an art since his was the first book I knew to be published by a Filipino about eskrima. I offer to him and his students, our great respect and good wishes.

PART 2

THE FOUNDATION OF THE ART

CHAPTER 3

PRELIMINARIES

Like any other martial art eskrima starts with stretches and warm ups to avoid muscle and ligament injury. Thereafter, a practitioner should understand the grip, stances, weight distribution, weight shift, balance and power strikes. Then he learns the 12 basic strikes—the target, safety precautions, facing the strike, the "hammerhead" feel and concept in striking. A beginning eskrimador should understand that the blade was part of the basis of earlier training for bolo fights thus the blade concept of slashing and slicing with the blade. I have discussed the "Buot Ball Concept" in catching and parrying strikes. This chapter addresses stick retraction to avoid control and capture of your stick by the opponent. We warn against telegraphing of strikes and address stick speed and velocity; training for "feel" and sensitivity to pressure and movement, peripheral vision and understanding hostile intent. We also have to have a basic understanding of other styles and other martial arts.

Warm-up Exercises

In Eskrima, warm up is crucial to avoid injury during training by loosening and stretching tight muscles and ligaments. Repeated strains on the ligaments could eventually lead to muscle spasms, rotator cuff injury, arthritic pain and/or torn ligaments. This could mean a lifetime of pain and suffering. So please, always start each training session gradually with warm ups to help avoid unnecessary injury. Let's look at how specifically to warm-up each area of the body as needed for Eskrima.

Wrists—Eskrima makes extensive use of the wrists. Wrist exercises are done by holding the stick in the middle and twisting it in a fan-like manner. Other warm up exercises include pressing the palms (fingers up) against each other or the back of the hands (fingers down) against each other in front of the chest. Push the fingers back and the thumb back alternately on each hand. Always begin slowly and build up gradually.

Arms—Raise your left arm above your head and pull the elbow toward the right. Alternate the exercise with the right arm and do the same motion. Next, keep the arms straight as you rotate both arms forward and backward from the shoulders to loosen joints.

Chest—Hold your hands behind your back and pull them until you feel your chest tighten. Next, hold your hands in front of your chest and push them against each other. After this, do push-ups to place more load on the arms and chest for strength and endurance.

Legs—Leg strength is connected with core strength, and also flexibility. For this, you can do sit ups, and stretches of the foot, legs, knees and hamstrings for flexibility.

Back—Lie flat on the floor and raise your butt while keeping your upper back flat on the floor. Another stretch is to raise one leg and pull it from behind the knee to feel a stretch in your hamstrings. Do each leg in an alternating manner. After this, slowly bend at the waist to touch the floor.

Neck—Rotate your neck slowly clockwise and counter-clockwise several times and then drop it forward and lift it up and backward several times. This should be done slowly. Do not snap suddenly.

Body—Do slow hip rotations. Keep the trunk steady while turning your upper torso alternately left and right with knees slightly bent. After this, stand in a shoulder width stance, bend forward at the hips and reach toward the floor. Also alternately, reach for opposite toes.

Proper Form

Stick Grip—Hold the stick about 1-inch from the butt in a firm (but not too tight) hammer grip—this is the same way you hold a hammer at the handle. This is the basic grip. The stick must be held at a 90-degree angle with your arm. Do not bend the wrist while striking. Avoid the limp wrist please! It is too unmanly.

Alternate gripping techniques will be discussed later, and are taught when the student understands the dangers of each situation and has further acquired the skill, speed and training to react in a fast and effective manner. For example, the danger of leaving a long butt (i.e., more space from your hand to the end of the stick) is the likelihood of being disarmed or controlled by the opponent; it is unwieldy; it shortens your weapon; and lessens your range advantage and leverage.

On-Guard Position—Some masters lean the stick on the side of their neck, or on their collarbone, while in fighting stance. Practitioners do this when they have the confidence, speed, and training. For proper posture, clip your elbows loosely and close to your side at a 90-degree angle. Forearms should be held in a horizontal position while the stick should be held in a vertical position. Avoid slanting the stick forward as it leaves the fighter open to being disarmed and open to an opponent's sneaking strike or sliding strike. The tip of the stick must be at level with the top of your head to cover strikes to the head, neck, and face. The left hand must be loose and ready for quick use, held close to the chin similar to a boxing guard.

The right foot should be forward at a distance of one regular walking pace. Avoid a wide and inflexible stance. Bend both knees slightly and raise your left heel slightly with the weight very slightly on the forward right foot (55-45% ratio) when delivering strikes. It is the athletic stance. Otherwise, the weight must be able to shift to either direction very quickly.

Use of Eyes—Although some martial arts look at their opponent's chest or the neck, in Balintawak we look straight into our opponent's eyes. We maintain eye-to-eye contact, with a keen eye (line of sight) for their hand and not their stick. We do this for the following reasons:

Do not attempt to follow the stick with your eyes as in watching a ping-pong game. Use peripheral vision and "feel" in sensing the stick and body movement and inertia.

Using peripheral vision to guard against attack with hands, feet and the stick in case of grappling and infighting. Guard against elbows knees and head-butts.

As part of the psychological warfare, to instill fear and intimidation, hesitation, panic and even terror and also to show confidence, resolve and determination this often unnerves a fainthearted foe.

Distance, Stepping and Balance

Fighting Distance—It is important to maintain the proper fighting distance between you and your opponent. The reasons are to keep your balance, deliver power strikes and maintain control over your opponent. This is achieved by proper stepping. The following are basic rules. They are not set out in concrete; but learn first the basics. When a fighter knows what he is doing, he may break the rules, often as a ruse to trap his unsuspecting foe into thinking he has an open strike. Let's look at this top when the stick is in motion and when the stick is not in motion.

When the stick is not in motion:

- If the opponent's right foot is forward, withdraw your left foot to maintain proper fighting distance.
- If opponent's left foot is forward, withdraw your right foot to maintain distance, avoid being stepped on or kicked. The same rule is true with your left foot.
- In the same manner, if the opponent withdraws his left foot, make a forward step with your right foot to maintain the proper fighting distance and to maintain control of your opponent.

When stick is in motion:

- If opponent's stick is on your left side, withdraw your left foot to avoid a "dropping strike." Do not turn your back to the strike; face it.

- If opponent's stick is on your right side, withdraw your right foot for the same reason and face the strike.

- If your opponent delivers a strike to your left side while your foot is withdrawn, do not withdraw your foot any farther. Instead, turn your left shoulder farther left and away from the blow to face the strike.

If your opponent delivers a strike to your right side while stepping backward, do not withdraw your right foot if it is in a forward position. Instead, step forward with your left foot to maintain control and proper fighting distance.

Note: Avoid double stepping or shuffling. Be precise, economical and, like a running back, be quick to shift directions while still maintaining balance in your movement. I see that even among other Balintawak groups, some have been careless in stepping and also double stepping.

Balance—One of the abiding principles of Balintawak Eskrima is balance and shiftiness. That is, maintaining balance on both feet with the ability to shift weight forward, backward or sideways, considering of course the physics and dynamics of power strikes. I liken this to the ability of a running back to change direction by faking a move and then moving in the opposite direction, or a boxer's ability to shift, dodge, weave or bob.

Effective delivery of strikes and effective defense against strikes, kicks or punches depends a great deal on balance. For this reason, Balintawak advocates normal balanced steps, short and low snap kicks and a balanced delivery of blows.

The late Balintawak Grandmaster Anciong Bacon always spoke of Center Balance. When the person is hit above his center of balance, his tendency is to fall backwards and when he is hit below his center of balance, the tendency is to fall forward. This is important to know, and keep in mind, while fighting an opponent so that you can use this information to your advantage.

CHAPTER 4

GENERAL PRINCIPLES AND EXERCISES

There are certain general principles that define the essence of Balintawak Eskrima in general, and the Buot Balintawak Eskrima in particular, that separate it from other styles. Some principles are generic in eskrima and martial arts as a whole. Some styles have different angles of strikes and the difference in the number of strikes and defenses. We have a reason for ours as they have justification for theirs. We will not argue their choices.

In power strikes, even within Balintawak, there is a variation of the "on-guard" and "ready position." Regardless, the important thing is not to telegraph the strike, notwithstanding the starting position of the strike. Withdrawal of the stick must be way before the strike. Unique to the Buot Balintawak Eskrima is the Ball Concept—the theory is that the stick speed cannot be parried fast enough if, as generally practiced, the strike is swatted across in right angle to the strike. Thus, the Buot Ball Theory is to catch the hand as if catching a fast ball, absorbing the power and deflecting the strike, as will be explained later. The process is involved and demands close and detailed execution.

Another theory unique to Balintawak, although unknown to those less observant of the masters, is the technique of capturing and controlling the stick. This is the essence of the kwentada method, often spoken of but very seldom and almost never understood. This is the magic of Anciong and Balintawak Eskrima. This was the technique that drove even advanced students apoplectic.

12 Strikes and Variations

Students must learn first to deliver the basic 12 strikes and then their variations. These consist of slashing strikes, hammer strikes, thrusts, horizontal strikes and flicking or fan strikes in combination with boxing blows, elbow strikes and kicks. Flicks are used more for exercise or distraction rather than as a power strike. It is also used in ruses. Regardless, if you are hit by any strike, it will sting. In doing the drills in this book, emphasis must be placed on power, balance and accuracy. I often belittled the flicking (witik) technique until I saw Nene Gaabucayan spit a coconut with one flick. Now I believe that with proper training, it can be an effective and powerful strike.

Face the Strike

Be sure to always face your opponent's strike is important. Even if you are struck at an oblique angle, turn your body to face the strike. This makes your block more solid and secure. I noticed Anciong do this as his signature move and characteristic.

Shadow Fighting

Practice delivery of strikes and thrusts with proper footwork in forward and backward motions. One way to practice is by hanging a string or small rope and tying a knot at the end of it. Practice hitting the knot from various angles and at different heights using power and keeping your balance. In the Philippines, where vegetation is lush, we would pick the tip of a particular leaf and practice hitting just the tip of that leaf from different directions or practice abrupt stops to practice stick control. Teddy Buot was a master of this.

Power Strikes

Power strikes are the result of a combination of proper weight shift, hip twist, shoulder and forearm contraction and expansion with wrist action, creating torque with the fullest speed at the point of impact. The greatest ripping power is at the tip of the stick. It will tear off the flesh. There is a "sweet spot" on the stick when delivering the blow for power strikes. The best impact point will be about from three-inches below the tip to about eight-inches from that point above the middle of the stick. Strike through the target for maximum power. A good power strike obtains maximum impact on contact and will end the fight abruptly. Work on it!

Whether you use the on-guard position described above or rest the stick on your shoulder is a matter of personal preference. Bobby Taboada prefers resting the stick on his shoulder before unleashing a powerful strike. Nene Gaabucayan can unleash tremendous power through wrist, shoulder and hip coordination. The important thing is not to telegraph by chambering or drawing back the stick before the strike. Learn all correct methods.

Bladed Weapon Concept for Stick

Traditionally, it was important to think of the stick as a machete, bolo or *pinute*. After all, the machete is substituted today with the rattan eskrima stick as a training tool for machete or bolo fighting. When striking with your stick you must imagine that you are slashing with the blade as you engage your point of contact. The blade of the imagined machete would be in line with the second digit of your gripping fingers. Regardless of the direction of the strike, the same rule applies. It must be remembered that the stick was used as a training tool to prepare for bolo duels. But with the main use of the stick these days, as a tool and as a weapon on its own, more surface area can be utilized to strike with. Since the stick is rounded, it can in fact strike at any surface; whereas with the bolo only the blade edge is for optimal use.

Regardless, stick training should coincide with blade concept. As such, at the end of the strike, it must be remembered that the striker must roll or pronate the wrist; otherwise, it will cause great strain and eventual damage on the wrist and elbow and even induce permanent injury. Thus in delivering strike number one, it is a palm up to palm down delivery upon full pronation. Correspondingly, a number two strike starts with a palm down start and ends up with the palm-up in ready position for the next strike. If you have a sand bag, you can practice striking this was on the bag. Also, you can place old tires of similar size on top the other and strike them with full power.

Exceptions: The exception to this striking concept is when executing a fan-strike (*abaniko*), flick strike (*paypay*), or thrust (*tusluk/dugsak*). Traditional Balintawak practitioners do not use *abaniko* as a power strike, although this has been demonstrated as an effective ruse or even as a power strike in the hands of an expert, as is the case with Nene Gaabucayan as mentioned above.

Hammerhead Concept and Feel

When striking allow the weight of the hammerhead to drop using gravity and momentum for power.

Berada – Telegraphing Your Strikes

In striking, do not pull back or swing the stick back before delivery of the strike as this is telegraphing your move. If you must pull back for power, do it before initiating the strike. Pulling back announces your move, and you lose valuable split second time in the delivery of the strike. This split second time loss means a lot in the hands of an expert. Obtain torque and power from the legs, hip, shoulder, forearm and wrist. This problem of telegraphing moves is precisely why the Balintawak masters were vehemently against the amara (shadow fighting).

Retracting the Stick

Another basic principle in delivering a strike is to retract the stick immediately after the strike. In other words, do not extend your hand, stick or any part of your anatomy to be within reach, touch or control of your opponent. This principle is followed also in empty-hand combat and knife fighting. An expert Balintawak practitioner can easily capture an opponent's stick upon contact. Thus, your weapon must immediately be retracted. My boast is: If I can touch your stick, I will disarm you.

The Buot Ball Concept

I call this as such since I think it is an innovation and want to place my charter claim and stake on it. I have not heard it discussed elsewhere. Think of the hand coming your way as you would in catching a strong fast ball. You cannot catch a fast ball by swatting it nor can you catch a fist by just parrying it. You cannot swat a ball sideways even at 80 miles per hour, much less at a 100 mph or more. You have to meet it and catch it. You catch the fist with your open palm and deflect the powerful fist or strike to avoid hurting your hand or absorbing the force and power of the strike. In the same manner a bullet, if it strikes directly on the side of the car, will penetrate the car but if it strikes the car at an angle, it will be deflected. In the same manner the power of the punch or the strike is deflected with this ball concept. As kids, we played skipping flat stones on the lake or sea. The principle is the same.

Stick Speed and Velocity

The stick is extremely fast. The slight flick of the wrist is magnified by the length of the stick. To elucidate on the magnification of the speed, imagine a powerful ray of light extending from the tip of your stick to the sky, the way those beams of lights from carnival shows sweep across tens of miles of sky. In a smaller scale, this illustrates the magnification of the speed: a four-to-six inch flick of the wrist could mean a magnification of six-to-eight feet.

Reflexive Reaction

Reflexive reaction is developed from repeated correct practice and presence of mind. If you are a panicky and anxious person, you are likely to react too early to a ruse, set-up or trick (*lansis*).

Controlling and Capturing Opponent's Stick

Whether doing a defensive or offensive move, your left hand must be in ready position to capture your opponent's stick or defend against a counter-strike. Thus, the left hand must follow both the strike and the defense, at all times. Capturing will start with a cupping habit for workouts and hooking for implementation and should progress to wrist and arm control. This slows down the opponent tremendously. This could be demonstrated during lessons. It is one of the secrets of control.

Using Peripheral Vision

Keeps your eye on the opponent and be keenly observant of his left hand. It is the Balintawak secret weapon! Do not follow the stick with your eyes. Use peripheral vision and a sense of touch in observing hand movement. Retract your stick immediately after delivering a strike. Never allow opponent to control your stick or even touch it. On the other hand, if you are on the defense, immediately control your opponent's stick, if possible. Making use of your peripheral vision will aid greatly in this skill.

Hikap – Touch and Feel

The concept of hikap, or touch and feel, is another area emphasized in Balintawak Eskrima. Another of Grandmaster Anciong Bacon's few English words terms was feeling. You should develop sensitivity and must feel inertia as to where your opponent's hand and body movements are directed. On contact with the opponent's striking arm/hand, you should feel pressure or slack. Feel and touch is an aid to what the eyes cannot see. With a highly developed sensitivity of feel and touch you can sense openings from the pressure, slack or release in the opponent's body or hand in contact with hand and/or stick. This will be covered more extensively in a later chapter.

Hostile Intent

In workouts, although strikes are controlled, there should be no misjudgment as to the purpose of the strike. It should target a designated area with the purpose of inflicting injury. Many eskrimadors merely "bang sticks" and this is not indicative of high skill. We should not bang sticks like children playing, playing Captain Sparrow or Captain Blood but rather target designated areas, especially the head, hands or closest part of the opponent's anatomy. Although we aim for a specific or designated target, we have to practice stick control to be able to stop the stick short of the target. The purpose of control in practice is obviously to avoid hurting our workout partner. Controlling the stick has been criticized by some as developing bad habits of aborted strikes. I say, you will quickly run out of workout partners without controls. I found Teddy Buot to be a great expert of this technique and stick control.

Abandoned Left Hand

If your opponent is controlling your left hand, as soon as he abandons control of that hand, use it for an offensive strike. It was my compadre Joe Villasin who enlightened me in this method of utilizing immediately the newly-free left hand to strike with, instead of leaving it where it is or for a block support. Like our slogan says, "It's all in the left hand."

Witik, Labtik, Abaniko, Pay-Pay

All of these technique terms are in the same category generally and are terms used interchangeably within Balintawak. They reflect the use of a flicking or snapping fan strike to any part of the opponent's body, done mostly by wrist action. As demonstrated by Nene Gaabucayan, who with one snap, can split a coconut which is about the same density as a skull. That is powerful.

Prepare for Other Styles

Prepare for fighting against other styles. Do not think that your opponent will strike or defend in the traditional basic forms or manner that you have trained within your style. There are a numerous styles with weird and peculiar strike forms and defenses that can puzzle and mystify you. There are reasons that we do not use those forms, but to master the art you must learn them to be able to defend against them. Understand the underlying principles of other fighting arts.

Demystifying the Amara Dance Style

This is purely for academic discussion. Balintawak purists will never be caught doing these zarzuela; they had a visceral dislike for these grandstanding dances. As I have suggested earlier, some younger masters in their effort to promote the art have adapted these elaborate moves in promoting their videos and seminars. For exercise and warm up, I will concede to its use. It can develop fluidity and grace of motion. It is the fancy and elaborate stick twirling, flicking, whipping, fan blows that look ornamental, circuitous and actually exhausting. It is also the signature move of old style 18th and 19th century ornate Eskrima that still finds currency in some styles. Watch old clips of old eskrimadors. It looks ridiculous and bizarre but yet it still finds currency among young eskrimadors.

While it is lavish and ornamental the amara adds little to eskrima's utilitarian value. It was and is used as an intimidation dance that actually exhausts the wielder! Balintawak eskrimadors are neither impressed nor intimidated by such grandstanding because Balintawak moves are practical, economical and effective. The idea is to conserve your energy for combat. Anciong and other Balintawak masters ridiculed it. As we have learned in grade school geometry, the shortest distance between two points is a straight line. This also applies to eskrima. Thus, avoid the circuitous showboating amara in a real fight.

Distance Fighting

Balintawak fighting largely emphasizes close quarters fighting. Of course the fight starts with distance fighting, starting with intimidation dances like the amara. This progresses to mid-range fighting and then moves on to close range fighting. Emphasis on close combat fighting is due to its effectiveness and dual use in empty and bare hand fighting. It must be remembered that the stick is just an extension of the arm.

Safety Caution

During practice and drills, thrusts to the eyes and even to the nipple are aimed outside the body area for safety to avoid injury. Safety cannot be over emphasized in practice and drill sessions. This warning will be repeated from time to time to remind the reader to avoid potential injury. An accidental thrust to the eyes can cause severe and permanent injury and even blindness and a thrust to the throat can be fatal. Please be careful.

CHAPTER 5

THE 12 BASIC STRIKING TARGETS

There are basic striking targets or angles used for training in class and then there are those targets used in actual combat. Experiment by holding a piece of paper. Hit it first with the middle of the stick, then hit it with the tip of the stick, see which one tears the paper. Also, feel the "sweet spot" as in striking a golf ball or baseball. In terms of the 12 strikes we utilize in Balintawak training, they are described and depicted below.

12 Strikes at a Glance

Strike Number 1—Right foot forward with weight slightly on the right foot, assuming the striker is right handed, with both knees slightly bent. Deliver the blow to the left side of the opponent's head. The grip starts with a palm-up grip with the stick in a vertical position and the strike ends with the palm-down. Clip close to the left side of your body. The stick is at 90-degree angle with your arm and remains at the same angle throughout the strike. Shift your weight to the left side as you complete the strike and to regain your balance quickly. Derive torque from the legs to the uncoiling of the upper torso through hip, shoulder, arm and wrists for an explosive strike. Remember the bladed concept with the blade-edge in line with the second digit of your fingers.

Strike Number 2—Side step to your left with most of your weight on your left foot. Grip your stick with your palm down. Start your slashing strike with the stick at about your left shoulder and ending at your opponent's right ear. Simultaneously shift your weight onto your right foot with the uncoiling of your upper torso for full force delivery. Regain balance quickly. The point of impact would again be as the blade of a machete slashing. The grip ends with palm up, finally resting in ready position right of center.

Strike Number 3—This is a strike to your opponent's right rib cage or to his elbow, if his arms are clipped, using the same principles described above in strike number 2.

Strike Number 4—Pivot your feet to face right. Resume the position as in strike number 1 by pivoting obliquely right. Deliver the blow to the opponent's left floating ribs or to his left elbow if his arms are clipped. Follow the same principle of power delivery, weight shift, and balance.

Strike Number 5—Step forward with your left foot. With your palm down and with the stick at 90-degree angle with your arm, thrust the stick toward the opponent's solar plexus (advanced variations to breastbone, throat, and groin. The wrist remains firm at 90-degrees. No limp wrists, please, and do not bend your thumb or point your finger forward. The thrust is done with a lunging movement. Again, obtain power from the leg thrust, torque from hip and shoulder, and use of an explosive twist of the body for optimum power.

Strike Number 6—Withdraw left foot and left shoulder into a sideways stance. With palm up and your stick at a 90-degree angle, thrust the stick below the opponent's right nipple. For beginners, remember earlier caution of aiming outside the body for safety. Again, this is done in a lunging manner with proper hip and shoulder movement.

Strike Number 7—Step your left foot forward into an oblique sideways stance and, with palm down, thrust the stick below the opponents' left nipple. (For drills and workout, thrust outside the body as in strike number 6, to avoid accident injury). Do this in the same lunging manner and with the same hip and shoulder torque, as in strike number 6.

Strike Number 8—Withdraw your left foot and bend your knees. Do not bend at the hips and drop your head forward, as this will get your hair and head within the opponents reach. With palm up, deliver a slashing strike to your opponent's left knee. Do not bend forward or you could be hit with a punch or your hair could be grabbed and pulled.

Strike Number 9—Pivot and sidestep to your left and with both knees bent, deliver a slashing strike to the opponent's right knee. Again, keep your hair and head away from the opponent's reach and remember to keep your eyes from being poked.

Strike Number 10—Withdraw your left foot as in Strike number 6. Stand sideways with your left shoulder drawn back. Do not over-rotate. Thrust outside the body to avoid injury especially the eyes. Your thrust must be with the palm-up position. Your arm must be at right angle with your stick. Of course in actual combat, the eyes are the target. For workouts this obviously cannot be the target. Safety must always be employed.

Strike Number 11—With left foot forward and palm down, withdraw right shoulder into a sideways stance and deliver a thrust to the opponent's left eye. Again, practice safety as in strike number 10.

Strike Number 12—This is a hammer strike to the opponent's head. Power is attained by the downward weight shift coordinated with the usual hip, shoulder, arm and wrist action in a downward chopping action. Again, the wrist remains firm at 90-degrees with your stick. Optimum speed and power should be at point of impact. The greatest ripping effect, however, is at the tip of the stick.

PART 3

THE DEFENSIVE STAGE

CHAPTER 6
BASIC DEFENSIVE CONCEPTS

In Balintawak Eskrima, great emphasis is placed on defense. As Bobby Taboada says, "The easiest thing to learn is how to hit but the most difficult thing to learn is how to defend." In the Buot Balintawak system I insist on a simultaneous counter-offensive, which is a simultaneous attack in conjunction with the defense. This was not specifically mentioned by Anciong Bacon but keen observation showed it was how he executed his moves sometimes. While he was defending a strike, he was already executing a counter-offensive. For instance, in a number one strike he would block the strike with an open palm and strike simultaneously the opponent's body with his stick. Most of us do it but are unaware of a hidden technique concealed in that simple move. You have to have been a keen student of Anciong to notice these techniques.

The student's first lesson is to defend himself and simultaneously make a counter offensive move. Like any sport, scoring is very important but defense is also important to keep the opponent from scoring on you. It is just unacceptable to be hit with a weapon. There are no gloves or protective gear in real Balintawak Eskrima. The slightest rap even on the fingers, knuckles and head can end the game. Offensive moves are immediately taught to prospective fighters who volunteer in a sparring match, pick-up fight or a tournament. A keen student, Adam Tompkins, had an epiphany and noted and observed what I was teaching. He called it a *counter-offensive move*, a term that I liked and have used since then. My revised version of the art is to knowingly use immediate, simultaneous counter-offensive moves. This will be a departure from the one-two strike and counterstrike method of the traditional way.

The best defense is a good offense. In the defensive stage, the student learns the basic defenses against the 12 basic strikes and their corresponding counter-strikes. Also taught are reflexive groups of movements that develop certain reflex responses under various situations.

The Buot Ball Concept Reviewed

As a preliminary statement, it must be remembered that a full power strike with the stick is difficult to block with a stationary stick. The force could be so strong that your stick could bounce off the opponent's stick and strike your own face or head. Thus, I advocate the application of what I have termed the Buot Ball Concept. Described below are the mechanics of the method, in which the counter-strike must be met with:

1. Match the Strike with Equal Force—The strike is met with an equal or superior force or power with your stick; otherwise, your stick must be cushioned with your forearm with your elbow tucked in, or with your palm heel or both, then: control the opponent's stick to clear by parrying it down. The term *control* has dual meaning and is another term for capturing the opponent's stick, a technique described elsewhere. This control and capture is the basis of my claim, "If I can touch your stick, I will disarm you."

2. Deflect the Strike—Apply the Buot Ball Concept by deflecting the strike in a glancing manner. Keep your eye on the ball, in this case his hand or fist. If your elbow is not tucked it, it will become a target and could end the fight for you.

3. Catch and Absorb the Strike—Anyone who has caught a strong baseball pitch or a strong football pass knows that it hurts your hand if you do not know how to absorb the power of a strong pass. The same is true in an eskrima strike.

Mechanics of the Buot Ball Concept—This technique is difficult to capture in words. It has to be demonstrated repeatedly with great attention to detail. In a bare hand punch, the defender "catches" the hand on the same side as the striking fist. First you "meet it," as in catching a ball, and then "deflect it," as in deflecting a flat stone on the lake. You must check and push the wrist of the opponent's attacking hand toward him, hooking his right hand and controlling the opponent's wrist. The defender grabs and jerks down the hand to break opponent's balance.

Mechanics of the Stick Defense Using the Ball Concept—The defender "catches" the fist with his open palm on the same side of the striking hand, and *simultaneously* strikes the striking hand with a slashing left to right strike.

Do not catch the stick! You must catch the hand. And your left hand must be in a ready position for the counter-offensive. With a slight crouch and your left hand close to your chin as in a boxing position, you are in the position to both defend yourself and go into an offensive move.

The touch of the stick is a very important training tool in Buot Balintawak Eskrima. This is the basis of control and timing of the fight. The beginner will not understand this completely until he advances in his training. It is part of the *tapi-tapi* (checking hand). It is one reason why Bacon opted for the one stick (*solo baston*) instead of the two sticks (*doble baston*) as in the old style eskrima.

CHAPTER 7

DEFENSES AGAINST 12 STRIKES

Practice safety during this drill. For practice, deliver thrusts outside the body to avoid accidental injury.

Defense: Strike Number 1

The student faces the strike and blocks the stick with equal or superior force. (In actual combat, the strike would be to the hand.) The forearm, palm heel or both should be behind his stick. The block is a semi-downward stroke with the stick held upright and at a right angle to the instructor's stick. The student's left hand should *simultaneously* control instructor's stick for a retaliatory strike. The operative word is *simultaneously*. This is a crucial move that will be explained later. The student twists his body to the left, with his body weight shifting mostly on his retracted left foot. The stick should be forming an X with the student's hand now touching near the end of the instructor's stick. *(see footnote 1)*

Footnote 1: For purposes of training, the student must not hold the instructor's stick, for reasons to be explained later. He must, however, feel the stick with his left hand. Anciong Bacon would rap a student that grabs his stick as a penalty for violating training instructions. The author's theory is that it delays the instructor's own reaction thus slows the sequence (*palakat*) and tempo, the instructor then loses control. This was never explained and discussed – only obeyed. Teddy Buot had a similar disciplinary rule: No explanation, only obey and follow!

In this position, the student clears the instructor's stick with his left hand in a downward motion. He delivers strike number two to the right side of the instructor's head. The student's weight should shift to his right foot upon completion of his blow. The shift has implications in obtaining a power strike. The student must proceed to regain his balance and retract his stick back to the starting and ready position.

Defense: Strike Number 2

The student again faces the strike and blocks the instructor's stick with a semi-downward slashing block, as he simultaneously withdraws his right foot. (In actual combat the strike would be to the hand.) The student's left hand should simultaneously control the instructor's stick for a retaliatory strike. The student twists his shoulders to the right and transfers his weight to his right foot, retaining balance. Both sticks should now be forming an X. The student's left hand should control instructor's stick and then clear it with a downward parry with his left hand.

After the student clears the instructor's stick, he delivers strike number 1 to the left side of the instructor's head. In delivering strike number 1, the student's body weight should shift to his left leg. He obtains torque power from the simultaneous weight shift, unwinding of the hip and shoulder, in coordination with the arm and wrist motion. The student then quickly regains his balance, retracts his stick and assumes the ready fighting stance. Student's right foot should be withdrawn to the rear.

Defense: Strike Number 3

This time the student does not block the instructor's stick but instead blocks the instructor's right wrist with his stick. The student's left hand is simultaneously transferred near the butt of

the instructor's stick with student's weight mostly on his right foot. The left hand transfer is for the student to feel and control the movement of the instructor's stick.

From this position, the student delivers a slashing number 1 strike to the left side of the instructor's head, maintaining the same position in both feet. Again, follow the same weight shift and body dynamic as described earlier. The student quickly retracts his stick and tries to regain his balance as he assumes a fighting stance with his right foot at the rear.

Defense: Strike Number 4

This has the same execution as strike number 1, except that the strike is lower, targeting the student's left elbow or floating ribs. The student's left foot is withdrawn. The student bends his knees while keeping his body straight and shifts his weight to his left side in order to obtain power in delivery of a retaliatory power strike. Further, this moves the student farther from a possible punch from the opponent's left hand. The student strikes the wrist and in practice blocks the stick. With both sticks forming an X, the student's left hand feels the stick for control.

From this position, the student clears the instructor's stick with a downward stroke of his left hand for a retaliatory strike number 2 to the right side of the instructor's head. Most of student's weight is transferred to his right foot upon delivery of this strike. He twists his body and shoulders in coordination with his arms and wrists to deliver his blow. Again, the student should immediately retract his stick to regain his balance and to avoid the opponent's control as earlier discussed.

Defense: Strike Number 5

The student parries with the similar execution as parrying strike number 1. Since the thrust (*totsada*) is lower, the student bends his knee, left foot at the back, in a firm and balanced position. (This is a thrust to the abdomen, with variations to the groin, solar plexus or the throat.) The student can evade the thrust in three ways:

1) By twisting and rotating his torso to the left to avoid the thrust. The twist narrows the target area and avoids the thrust. Student's weight should fall mostly on his left foot to avoid being within reach for a punch, butt-end strike or eye poke. *(see footnote 2)*

Footnote 2: Do not over-rotate and turn your back to the opponent. Weight should be on your left foot, balanced, body slightly lowered. If the weight is on your right, you will be drawn closer to your opponent within distance for hair pulling or a punch. Keep eyes focused on your opponent and not on the stick. As an instructor, upon delivery of a number 5 thrust, I reach out with my left to make sure the student is out of my reach. I usually jab his shoulder with my open palm to show that he was within a punch or an eye jab.

2) The student blocks the instructor's stick with his stick, point up.

3) Simultaneous with the stick block and evasive body twist, the student parries the stick with a scooping in and out movement with his left hand, the palm facing out and his fingers pointing downward. This will require some practice.

The student then clears the instructor's stick with his left hand and proceeds to deliver strike number 2. Again, the student should not hold on to the instructor's stick, as previously explained. Also, remember to shift your weight to attain optimum power delivery, balance and grace.

Defense: Strike Number 6

This has the same execution as in parrying strike number 2. The instructor's left foot must be withdrawn and student's right foot must be withdrawn with his weight on his right foot to retain balance. The student must make an emphatic twist back toward his right shoulder without turning his back to the instructor. The body turn avoids the thrust and narrows the target area. (Be careful not to move within the reach of your opponent as he could grab your hair or hit you with a punch. To avoid this, be sure your weight falls on your right foot as you twist your body.)

After blocking the thrust with his stick, the student clears or parries the instructor's stick downward with his left hand. The student delivers strike number 1, a slashing strike to the left side of the instructor's head. Again, remember the basics in weight shift from right to left, retracting the stick after the blow delivery and keeping the eyes on the instructor and not on his stick.

Defense: Strike Number 7

This has similar execution as the defense against strike number 1. Except that, this is a thrust. There is an emphasis on a sharp twist of the left shoulder to elude and escape the thrust as well as to narrow the target area, as earlier explained. Again, transfer your weight to your left foot as you turn sideways, to avoid falling within the reach of your opponent.

Simultaneous with your twist, block the instructor's stick with a semi-downward slashing strike. Your left hand should be ready to clear, parry and control the weapon. The student now delivers strike number 2. Again, follow all basics in strike delivery, including weight transfer, retracting your stick, and keeping your eye on opponent's eyes.

Defense: Strike Number 8

The student's left foot is back and steps right foot forward to reach the instructor's striking hand. Student bends both knees since the target is his left knee, but does not bend forward otherwise his hair will be grabbed or he will be within punching or eye poking range.

The student's left palm heel blocks the instructor's hand as he simultaneously strikes the instructor's forearm or elbow with his stick. Student's left hand should be below his stick. The student proceeds to deliver strike number 1 to the left side of the instructor's head, applying the usual fundamentals previously described.

Defense: Strike Number 9

With the student's right foot withdrawn, the student bends both knees without bending forward. His eyes should be fixed on the instructor's eyes or chest with peripheral observation of the movement of the stick. Never follow the stick with your eyes.

The student steps forward with his left foot, slightly toward the instructor's back. This is done to be closer to the instructor, to have better control, and to be away from any retaliatory blow. The student's left palm heel blocks the instructor's hand, close to the grip, as he simultaneously strikes the instructor's elbow. The strike will be above his left hand. The student then proceeds to deliver strike number 2. Follow all fundamentals of delivery of strikes.

Defense: Strike Number 10

The counter is similar to the counterstrike to strikes numbers 2 and 3, except that this is a thrust to the right eye. The student should do an emphatic right shoulder twist with the corresponding head movement away from the thrust while keeping his balance. His weight should be transferred to his right foot and his eyes are on the instructor. The student should not over-rotate and his right foot should never go beyond the center of his body. The student then

clears the instructor's stick with his left hand in a downward manner and proceeds to deliver strike number 1, observing all fundamentals of blow delivery.

Defense: Strike Number 11

The block is similar to strikes number 1 and 4. Remember this is a thrust to the left eye instead of a slashing blow. The student again pulls his left shoulder back with his weight transferred to his left foot. His head should also move in an evasive manner away from the thrust, although keeping his eyes on the instructor, meanwhile, maintaining his balance. The student then clears his instructor's stick in a downward stroke with his left hand and proceeds to deliver strike number 2, still observing all fundamentals of blow delivery.

Defense: Strike Number 12

This is a hammer strike to the head. The counter to this strike is unique and involved. It carries many implications and applications, and is a very important counter in bare hand combat and knife fighting. There are three ways the student may evade and defend against the blow:

1) The student ducks the strike, moving his head left and forward. Avoid the natural tendency to pull the head backward.

2) The student "catches the ball" by parrying the instructor's fist (not the stick or the arm). The power is absorbed and deflected to your right and outward, if you are right handed. The student controls the base of the instructor's stick with his thumb, his four fingers latch on the inside on the instructor's thumb to keep the instructor's stick from going wild and hitting the student's head.

3) The student delivers a simultaneous slashing strike number 2 to the instructor's wrist. This is a full strike with full power derived from the uncorking of the hips, shoulder, arm and wrist. The then student jerks the instructor's hands with his weight behind his pull; dropping down toward his right rear foot, using both his hands and body weight. He simultaneously withdraws his right foot and transfers his weight to his right foot. This breaks the opponent's balance.

The student transfers control by his left hand to the instructor's wrist, in front of the student's stick. This is done to free his stick and remove the obstruction for a full power strike. The student proceeds to deliver a strike number 1 to instructor's head, following all fundamentals of strike delivery for optimum power.

CHAPTER 8

COUNTER DEFENSES AGAINST 12 STRIKES

Counter Defense: Strike Number 1— Student blocks and delivers his counterstrike to instructor's strike number 1. With his right foot forward, the instructor blocks the student's stick with his stick pointing upward. The instructor simultaneously controls the student's stick near the butt on top of his left hand. The instructor exercises control to avoid a wild, unintentional and unexpected strike or move by the student. This is also done to slow the student's response thereby giving a chance to guide the student's hand with the parry. It is very important for the instructor to get a feel for the student's movement. In this position, the instructor releases his left-handed control of the student's stick as he proceeds to deliver strike number 2. Instructor then sidesteps to the left.

Counter Defense: Strike Number 2— Student blocks and delivers his counterstrike to instructor's strike number 2. The instructor's left foot is withdrawn as he simultaneously blocks the student's stick with his stick pointing upward. The instructor controls the student's stick (on top and toward the end) with his left hand. The instructor then guides the student's stick to his right side by shifting his left-hand control to face palm up, (inserted between the cross of the sticks and student's hand), then lifts the student's stick to his right side, making sure it clears the instructor's head. Simultaneously, the instructor delivers strike number 3 and sidesteps left with his left foot.

Counter Defense: Strike Number 3— Student blocks and delivers his counterstrike to instructor's strike number 3. The instructor withdraws his left foot further left and blocks student's stick with his stick. The instructor controls, with his left hand, the students stick toward the end of the stick from point of contact. The instructor then guides the student's stick with the back of his right hand over the instructor's head as he delivers strike number 4, while his foot remains withdrawn to the back.

Counter Defense: Strike Number 4— Student blocks and delivers his counterstrike to instructor's strike number 4. With his right foot forward, the instructor blocks the student's stick with his stick. The instructor controls the student's stick near the grip or butt of the stick, then releases control with his left hand and shifts control. With his palm facing down, he lifts the student's stick with the back of his left hand and arm, making sure the student's stick is controlled by his forefinger and thumb. The instructor then steps left foot forward while delivering strike number 5.

Counter Defense: Strike Number 5— Student blocks and delivers his counterstrike to instructor's strike number 5. The instructor, with his left foot still forward, blocks the student's stick with his stick. With his left hand, the instructor controls the student's stick with his hand toward the end of the stick from point of contact. With weight on his right foot, the instructor releases control of his left hand and delivers a number 6 strike as he withdraws his left foot and keeps weight on his right foot.

Counter Defense: Strike Number 6— Student blocks and delivers his counterstrike to instructor's strike number 6. The instructor blocks the students' stick with his stick and controls the stick (as in parrying strike number 2). With his left foot steady at the back, the instructor releases his left-hand control and pushes the stick towards the student's chest, as if to pin his stick on his chest. The instructor simultaneously delivers strike number 7 while simultaneously side stepping to the left, shifting his body weight onto his left foot.

Counter Defense: Strike Number 7—Student blocks and delivers his counterstrike to instructor's strike number 7. Instructor parries the counterstrike as in strike number 2, then releases control of the student's stick and bends his knees, keeping his body straight, to deliver strike number 8, a slashing strike to student's left knee. The student steps his right foot forward to the right, bends his knees, making sure not to bend over (as previously explained, this places him in danger), then blunts the strike by blocking the instructor's hand (not the stick) near the butt, with his palm heel and strikes instructor with strike number 1.

Counter Defense: Strike Number 8— Student blocks and delivers his counterstrike to instructor's strike number 8. Instructor parries student's counterstrike as in counters to strike numbers 2 and 3, except that the instructor has to lower his body by bending his knees to parry the strikes effectively. His left foot remains at the back and his body weight is mostly on his left foot. The instructor then releases his left-hand control, pivots facing oblique left on his bent knees, and slips his left hand palm up and flips the student's stick to his right side. He is careful to avoid not to catching his head with the student's stick as he proceeds to deliver strike number 9.

Counter Defense: Strike Number 9— Student blocks and delivers his counterstrike to instructor's strike number 9. Instructor blocks and delivers counterstrike with more pronounced bent knees, left foot still in a side step position to the left. Instructor then releases his left-hand control, stands up, withdraws his left foot, pulls his left shoulder back and delivers a number 10 strike.

Counter Defense: Strike Number 10— Student blocks and delivers his counterstrike to instructor's strike number 10. The instructor blocks the counterstrike as in blocking strike number 2, except that instructor's left foot is still withdrawn with his bodyweight mostly on his right foot. The instructor then releases his left-hand control and pushes the student's stick with his left hand to pin the stick on student's chest and proceeds to deliver strike number 11.

Counter Defense: Strike Number 11— Student blocks and delivers his counterstrike to instructor's strike number 11. The instructor blocks the counterstrike as if countering strike number 1, except that his left foot remains in that forward, oblique side step position. The instructor firmly pushes student's stick downward to make clearance for a number 12 hammer strike to the head.

Counter Defense: Strike Number 12—Student blocks instructor's hand and proceeds with the defense and proceeds to deliver a similar strike number 12. The instructor proceeds to close and control student's stick by grabbing the student's stick to hischest to control both his stick and student's stick, ending the basic *abecedario* series.

Definition of Control Terms

These two terms will be used extensively later in the book. They are terms I have developed for controls usually done simply through experience and common sense, instead of spoon fed education.

Outside Control – When blocking a strike, control outside the X of your crossing sticks; in the space above opponent's hand, toward tip of stick.

Inside Control – When blocking a strike, control inside the X of your crossing sticks; in the space between the sticks and opponent's hand.

Notes on Proper Drilling Method:

a) The lesson on blocking the counterstrike of the student by the instructor should be repeated in an orderly sequence, from strike number 1 to 12, repeatedly until mastered and embedded in the student's reflexes and muscle memory.

b) Then the instructor delivers strikes and thrusts at random, that is, out of the continuous 12 strike sequence. This stage is called *palakat*, the random stage.

c) After acquiring the skill, speed and correct execution of the lessons in the above drills, the student can proceed to training reflexes by grouping of movements, as described in the next section below.

CHAPTER 9
TRAINING REFLEXES BY GROUPING OF MOVEMENTS

In this section are presented the groups or a series of exercises to develop quick reflex exchanges in various given situations. The basis of these grouping exercises was developed by the late GM Jose V. Villasin, also a student of the grandmaster, Venancio "Anciong" Bacon. Some of Anciong's "purist" students dismiss this idea and consider this type of training as alien to the original training. That is correct as this is an innovation by the late Villasin. It was Villasin's brilliant idea to organize the general group of movements into varying sequences to help the students develop reflex responses to offensive strikes from any direction—either by lifting and clearing, thrusting, butting, developing body reflex, abaniko or fan strikes, and boxing, etc. Certain recurring situations call for varied responses and a projection or anticipation of counter responses. Thereafter, students were taught various optional responses to given situations and then given an arsenal of responses or moves. For the moment, students were taught these basic moves. Constant and correct repetition and practice leads to quicker reflex response.

The Grouping System is extensively seen on the net as the epitome of the Balintawak system. Unfortunately, there is much more. Villasin had other advance moves which he kept for control and which many do not know or refuse to acknowledge as existing. This was a source of consternation within the club as a form of favoritism. It was Villasin's call and decision who he would favor. He never revealed who shared his secrets. You could only tell by their moves.

Based on the same concept of grouping, with no intent of disrespect or of taking away from Villasin's original concept, I modified the groups by adding a few additional moves to elucidate the theory further. The Grouping Method as taught by Villasin has been in practice for the last 35 years and knowledge is expanding and growing in geometric proportions, thus the need for growth. Additional strikes; punches left and right, high and low; thrusts previously uncovered from both sides, high and low; fan strikes high and low; bobbing and weaving, slipping and *puño* (butt end strikes); pushing and pulling that has not been addressed earlier, etc. are now added in Group VI. Villasin made Anciong's theory easier to grasp without any disrespect to the Grandmaster and in the same manner, I find that the moves needed additional innovation, again without disrespect for my teachers. Like a good father, the objective of teaching is to teach, build and produce students who are better than their teacher or who can improve and develop the art. I hope to develop students better than me and who will, in turn, improve my teachings.

Group I: Lifting, Clearing, Trapping, Chopping, Slapping Down, Slapping Up

In Group I the student is taught to slap down or lift and clear the instructor's left hand. This is Anciong's signature move. We are assuming under these instructions that the opponent is right handed. This has to be adjusted if the opponent is left handed. It is not much different. The same principles apply, except that you are dealing with a different hand.

The instructor delivers strike number 1, which student blocks by crossing the instructor's stick.

The instructor simulates a control hold with his left hand over student's stick. Instructor lowers his hand and student's stick at about waist level.

The student lifts the instructor's left hand with student's left hand for an unobstructed and clear strike. The student strikes number 3 to instructor's left side. The instructor blocks the counterstrike with his stick in a vertical position.

As instructor clears the stick over head as he simultaneously guides it with the back of his left hand, with his thumb as a guide.

Instructor controls the student's stick on his grip at his left side.

Student lifts the instructor's left hand and delivers strike number 4 to the left side of instructor's body.

Instructor blocks the blow with a downward stroke of his stick while obliquely twist left, facing the stick to block it.

Student pins instructor's hand and stick on instructor's chest and delivers strike number 12 to instructor's head.

Instructor steps back with his weight onto his left foot and quickly frees his left hand and guides the strike over his head towards his right.

Instructor proceeds to deliver strike number 12 to student's head. Student guides the strike over towards his right.

Student delivers a number 12 counter strike to instructor's head.

Instructor delivers a number 1 strike.

Student counters with a strike number 2 to the instructor's face.

Instructor takes control of student's stick and flips it over to his left side, palm facing up.

Student slaps down and clears, deliver a strike number 1 to instructor's face.

Instructor flips over the student's stick to open up student's right leg and simultaneously delivers a strike number 9. Student drops his stick on instructor's right wrist to block the strike, while simultaneously controlling instructor's wrist with his webbed hand.

Student delivers strike number 2 to instructor's head. Instructor blocks the strike with his stick in a vertical manner to control student's stick, palm up towards left. Instructor blocks and controls both sticks to close Group I.

Group 2: Butting, Ducking, Slipping, Bobbing and Weaving

In Group II is designed as an exercise to develop quickness in ducking, bobbing and weaving of the head as boxers do. Bobbing is the up and down motion of the head with simultaneous bending of the knees. Weaving is the motion of going left to right and back in a U-shape motion, also with the bending of the knees and the waist. Slipping is evading a punch buy moving the head either left or right as the punch comes. This is also used to train the eyes in reacting to attacks or strikes to the face. Upon mastering Group I, the student proceeds to Group II. As the instructor closes Group I:

Instructor delivers strike number 6. Instructor faces obliquely left with his weight transferred mostly to his right foot as he delivers the thrust.

Student faces and blocks the stick, his eyes fixed on the instructor and clears the stick down with his left hand and delivers strike number 1.

Instructor blocks student's stick, controls the student's hand with his left hand.

Instructor withdraws his own stick under his elbow, allowing the student to lift and clear his left hand.

Instructor executes a butting strike to right side of student's body, which student blocks by dropping his left forearm.

Instructor controls student's hand and proceeds to butt to student's face, which student blocks with his palm heel.

Student slides the back of his left hand under the instructor's hand and stick, then guides both hand and stick over to students' left side. In so doing student must make sure that instructor's stick is in the web of his left hand, otherwise the instructor's stick could catch and hit his face.

Student clears instructor's left hand and controls it toward instructor's left hand.

Student delivers a boxing blow with his right fist to instructor's face. Instructor parries by catching student's open fist, deflecting the strike and guiding it over to his right side, as student weaves to his left.

Instructor proceeds to strike a number 12.

Student parries it down with his weight on his right foot and…

Student delivers strike number 1.

Instructor crosses to block outside and to control downward the student's stick.

Instructor slashes across student's head from left to right, or alternately strikes a number 2.

Student ducks forward and right, bending at the waist.

Instructor lifts student's left hand and strikes a number 1.

Student blocks number 1 strike.

Instructor controls student's stick downward and delivers a slashing number 1 strike, which student slips by leaning and weaving forward and left.

Instructor controls student's stick downward and delivers a slashing number 1 strike, which student slips by leaning and weaving forward and left.

Student parries instructor's hand down and delivers a number 1 strike.

Instructor quickly faces right and blocks with his stick, as instructor controls and closes Group II by controlling both sticks.

Group 3: Thrusting and Twisting

This group of movements is designed to drill the student in quickness and flexibility in shoulder and hip twists (*takilid*), both the right and left, to avoid thrusting or stabbing moves. These exercises are done along with Groups I and II, beginning from the closing of Group II.

Instructor delivers strike number 6, targeting the shoulder area to force the student to turn his shoulders.

Student twists his body facing the stick but keeping his eyes on the instructor's eyes and not on the stick.

Student's left hand controls instructor's stick (on top of the butt end) and clears it in a downward motion as in parrying strike number 2, and counters with a strike number 1.

Instructor blocks and crosses student's stick, the controls and substitutes the stick with his left hand, palm down, and delivers a strike number 7 to the left shoulder, again to force student to twist his shoulder farther left to avoid the thrust.

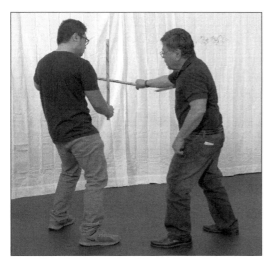

Student twists his body farther left, keeping his eyes focused on the instructor's eyes, simultaneously blocking instructor's stick with his stick.
(see footnote 1)

Student twists his body farther left, keeping his eyes focused on the instructor's eyes, simultaneously blocking instructor's stick with his stick.
(see footnote 1)

Student delivers strike number 2, which the instructor blocks with his stick and, with his left hand, controls student's right hand.

Instructor pushes the student's stick with the back of his left hand and forearm to open up the student for strike number 5.

Footnote: This is basic training. This rule may be broken in the advanced stage where you may submit yourself as open for an attack, as a ruse for an intended strike. This is known as the kwentada, which will be discussed in a later chapter.

Student twists and rotates his torso to his left to avoid the thrust, accompanied by a downward, palm-out scoop with his left hand. Student simultaneously blocks instructor's stick with his stick (point up).

Student proceeds to deliver strike number 3.

Instructor controls and thrusts over student's stick as student blocks and guides instructor's stick to his left side.

Instructor does a right to left cabra ripping strike, leading with the tip of the stick over student's stick.

Student weaves back and right and guides instructor's stick with his left hand.

Student strikes number 1.

Instructor blocks and thrusts number 10.

Student controls instructor's hand to slow down strike as he blocks the thrust. Student parries instructor's stick down and strikes a number 1.

Instructor blocks, parries down, and thrusts number 11.

Student blocks and strikes number 2 as instructor blocks the strike to close Group III.

Group 4: Stabs and Fan Strikes

This group of exercises is designed to drill the student in twisting and body flexibility, teaching him to turn his shoulders to evade a stab or a strike. Group IV follows from the cross and close of Group III.

The instructor delivers a thrust number 6.

Student blocks facing right.

Instructor controls outside and thrusts a number 7 to student's left side.

Instructor guides his stick with his left hand as he thrusts across his body toward student's right side in a ripping thrust, tip first (cabra).

Student counters by lifting the tip of his stick together with the instructor's hand toward his right.

Student guides the instructor's stick to his right, outside of his body, by lifting and directing student's left hand and stick, including instructor's stick, to his right. Student simultaneously rotates his shoulder to the right and transfers his weight mostly onto his right foot.

Student guides the instructor's stick to his right, outside of his body, by lifting and directing student's left hand and stick, including instructor's stick, to his right. Student simultaneously rotates his shoulder to the right and transfers his weight mostly onto his right foot.

Student pushes instructor's hand down to clear for a number 1 strike.

Instructor crosses the student's stick with his left hand on top.

Instructor releases control of his left hand to deliver a flicking fan strike, palm up, to student's left shoulder.

Student turns his left shoulder and backs the strike. Before student could deliver a counter strike, instructor transfers control by his left hand on top of student's stick to deliver another fan blow to student's right shoulder, forcing the student to turn his right shoulder and pursue (paapas) the strike with his counter. Student's weight falls mostly onto his right foot.

Student catches up to block and clear downward the strike to deliver strike number 1. Instructor blocks student's stick and controls student's stick with a downward left-hand parry.

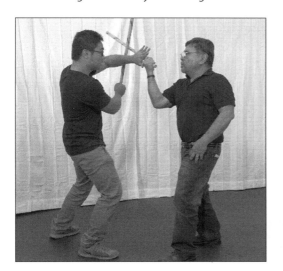

Instructor withdraws his left foot, with weight mostly on his right foot, weaves his head so that his stick does not catch his head and face. Instructor delivers another high fan strike to the left side of the student's head. Student turns his left shoulder, weight on his left foot, to face the strike.

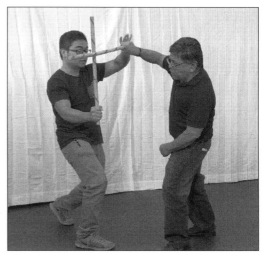

Instructor flips his stick to deliver a high fan strike to the right side of student's head.

Student delivers a number 1 strike as instructor blocks to close Group IV.

Group 5: Boxing, Parrying and Blocking Punches and Hammer Strikes

This group of exercise moves is used to develop reflexive response to boxing blows to the face and body during the trading of strikes and blows in conjunction with the stick. It follows sequentially from the end of Group IV.

Instructor delivers thrust number 6.

Student counters as instructor blocks and controls.

Instructor delivers thrust number 7 on the opposite side of student's body.

Instructor delivers thrust number 7 on the opposite side of student's body.

Instructor controls student's fist downward with a tanday movement (laying his fist on top of opponent's hand to pin the hand and keep it in check) and delivers a left uppercut under the student's right elbow.

Student drops his elbow to block, instructor still controls student's hand.

Instructor delivers a punch above student's arm towards his mid-section. Student raises his right elbow to deflect and redirect the punch with a stop to control a wayward or strong fist with his open palm heel, shifting his weight onto his left foot.

Instructor throws a left punch to student's face (use an open palm for workouts).

Student raises his right elbow and catches the fist with his open left hand.

Student clears instructor's right hand.

Student butts instructor's face, which instructor blocks and ducks forward and right, and delivers a right uppercut to student's left side.

Student drops left forearm to defend.

Instructor delivers a high butt strike to student's face and head, which student blocks with his forearm.

Student lifts instructor's controlling hand and executes a number 1 strike.

Instructor blocks, turning left to face the strike.

Instructor controls student's left hand and strikes a number 9 to student's right knee.

Student strikes a number 2 and instructor blocks to close Group V.

Group 6: Pushing, Pulling, Reverse Control, Jerking Down, Slipping and Balance

I have included this group as recognition of a move in Balintawak that has not properly been addressed earlier. It was a move of Grandmaster Bacon and Villasin but was not addressed as a separate group of moves. As previously, Group VI follows after the last move of Group V.

Instructor thrusts a number 6, with outside control, as student turns his right shoulder and blocks.

Instructor makes sure he transfers his stick to his right to push student's left shoulder more easily.

Student turns his left shoulder backward left to slip the push as his left hand slips instructor's left hand out. Student grabs instructor's hand.

Instructor reverses control and jerks student's arm across to instructor's left side.

Instructor strikes a number 1, and does a tanday, which student blocks facing the strike.

Instructor pushes student's right shoulder while student steps back with his right foot and blocks the push by raising his right elbow.

Student butts instructor's face as instructor ducks and flips stick to his left side.

Student butts instructor's face as instructor ducks and flips stick to his left side.

Student butts instructor's face as instructor ducks and flips stick to his left side.

Student strikes a number 4, which instructor blocks.

Instructor controls student's left wrist as he strikes a number 8.

Students clears instructor's left hand and strikes a number 1.

Instructor blocks and strikes a number 9 to close Group VI.

There are many more variations that can be done within the Grouping Movement Drills. These include practicing mini drills for slipping, bobbing and weaving, and rotating to slip strikes and thrusts. There are variation on where to strike, differentiating classroom drills and combat use. All in all, though, these series of drills presented in this chapter comprise the core training method of Balintawak Eskrima, and should be viewed and practiced as such.

PART 4

THE OFFENSIVE STAGE

CHAPTER 10

FIGHTING PRINCIPLES AND STRATEGIES

All things being equal between two fighters, the bigger and stronger person should win. With this also comes physical fitness, strength and stamina. However, nothing is ever equal. As such, the eskrimador must stack to his advantage as many things as possible. The following fighting principles and strategies will help you stack the deck in your favor.

First Strike

If you must fight, hit first if possible and hit hard enough to end the fight. In eskrima even a simple hit to vital points could end the fight—e.g., a rap hit to the fingers, wrist, eye, knuckles and face can immediately stun an opponent allowing you to move in for a good finish.

Strike the Closest Target

Strike the body part closest to your reach as opportunity presents itself. Hit the most convenient, open, favorable and direct spot or area. Remember the physics principle that the shortest distance between two points is a straight line. Watch especially for openings between the opponent's fist, stick and body.

Largo Mano — Long Range Fighting

At first encounter, the fight will probably start as a long distance encounter. It will probably start with intimidation dances of the *amara* style. The initial stage is a very crucial stage of the fight. Some styles specialize only in *largo mano* and call their style such. For some reason some Balintawak teachers calls some long distance strikes as *corto, a* misnomer which actually means short, probably for the shortened or truncated strikes. Inevitably, if the fighter knows what he is doing, if no part of the anatomy is hit, the fight will eventually end in sticks clashing, then the close combat fighting. When the sticks clash, you may proceed to close combat fighting for which Balintawak is noted. Close combat fighting is more sophisticated, refined and complicated and more than just the initial confrontational stages of the fight. *Largo Mano* is under the assumption that the fight ends at distance fighting, which in many instances it does.

Medio — Medium Range Fighting

This is based on the principle of hitting the nearest part of his body, probably explaining the word *corto,* meaning short in Spanish for the shortened or clipped strikes. This is confusing since I am talking of medium range fighting yet using the term *corto* for medium range. *Corto* is the name of the strike at medium or even long range, a strike that is shortened to hit the hand.

1. After a defensive cross on your right, shift his stick to your left and strike his left hand if it is near or strike the weapon hand (right hand holding his stick) in a right to left slashing strike.

2. After a defensive cross on your right, control his stick above the cross and strike his hand in a left to right slashing strike.

3. After a defensive cross on your left, shift his stick to your right with your control under the cross and strike his hand with a left to right slashing strike.

4. Apply advanced stepping, by stepping to the side and forward, weight forward and facing your opponent.

5. *Pabanda,* that is, after his full strike, cross and simply bounce your stick back to his head. This is achieved by a quick body and shoulder shift.

6. *Cabra* is a ripping strike. After his full strike, cross and bounce back with a ripping thrust, tip first instead of the slashing strike.

7. Strike the front leg if his weight is on it and proceed with other techniques.

8. If your opponent does the *amara*, apply your counter as described elsewhere.

Read Your Opponent's Background

More often than not, you can read your opponent's fighting background from his stance. A loose, mobile stance with flicking fast jabs followed by a cross could signal a boxer or a fighter with mostly hand skills, possibly a Muay Thai artist. A stiff, wide stance could signal a karateka or an art with dominant foot techniques. A person who rushes in and tries to grapple or go for your legs would most likely be a wrestler/grappler and should be handled accordingly. He could possibly be unskilled or could be a barroom brawler. Try to read give-away or telegraphed messages on how he will fight, and then fight accordingly. Recall immediate basic defenses instantaneously. In all instances, never under estimate the opposition, which does not necessarily mean that you do not have confidence in your own style or that you fight in fear.

Stepping Principles

1st Principle – As your opponent delivers a strike on your left side, your left foot must be withdrawn and your weight should be on your back left foot, as you counter with strike number 2. On the cross of your sticks, be quick to withdraw your right leg. Reason: To avoid being within easy reach and to avoid the drop shot or *patagak*.

2nd Principle – As you opponent delivers strike on your right, withdraw your right leg and transfer your weight on your withdrawn right leg. Counter with strike number 1. As he crosses to block, again be quick to withdraw your left leg to avoid being within easy reach of the drop shot.

3rd Principle – If you deliver a strike to your opponent's left side, and your opponent's weight is on his forward right foot, shift your strike to his right leg, as in long distance fighting. If you deliver a strike to your opponent's left side (your right side) and his left foot is forward with his weight on it, hit his left leg. He cannot retract it. Even if he is about to deliver a strike to your left, if his weight is on his forward left leg, shift the strike to his left leg. Note: The manner of hitting the forward leg, on which his weight is on, depends on whether your stick is under or over his stick.

4th Principle – Counter to Tripping. As your opponent trips your right leg with a simultaneous push on your body, counter by withdrawing your left leg backward and counterclockwise. Bend your right knee and transfer your weight to your right. Push with your right hand.

Dynamics in Balancing

Help the opponent shift his weight in a specific direction by pushing him. Also remember the general martial arts rule that where the head goes, the body follows. If the opponent counter-pushes, reverse the direction of your push using his momentum against him. Move his head away from the perpendicular line to his front foot (i.e., the attack position). Break his balance by pushing and pulling. If the opponent's weight is on his back foot, then he is not in the attack position but on the defensive. Caution: In that position however, watch for a snap kick with his front foot.

When balance is broken, deliver a strike or technique as this is when the opponent is least able to defend and there is an unobstructed opportunity to strike or apply a technique. Maintain your own balance and keep your ability to shift your position and direction. This is the essence of eskrima. The English word that most often came out of the grandmaster's mouth, was balance.

Hikap — Developing a Sense of Touch or Feel

The concept of *hikap*, or "touch and feel," is another area emphasized in Balintawak Eskrima. Another of Grandmaster Anciong Bacon's few English words was "feeling." You should develop sensitivity and must feel inertia to perceive where your opponent's hand and body movements are directed. On contact with the opponent's striking arm/hand, you should feel pressure or slack. Feel and touch is an aid to what the eyes cannot see. With a highly developed sensitivity of feel and touch you can sense openings from the pressure, slack or release in the opponent's body or hand in contact with hand and/or stick. Below are descriptions of the four principles of *hikap*, or "feeling."

1st Principle – When your opponent controls your stick through a sense of touch and feel, you should be able to determine by feel where to control or touch in response to reposition yourself to a superior controlling situation. This is developed by *experience*, *practice* and *awareness*.

2nd Principle – When you lift or take your hand away from controlling your opponent's stick, substitute your stick as a means of controlling his stick. The same is true in the reverse. In other words, when you lift your stick to strike, substitute your hand to control the opponent's hand, arm or stick. *Always maintain control of your opponent's stick.*

3rd Principle – Always be alert of your opponent's hand or stick pressure. Use his pressure or weight by reversing your position to take advantage of his strength and momentum; thus destabilizing his balance or upsetting his timing. For example, as your opponent clears your stick after a cross block against the number 1 strike, use his own force and momentum to deliver your strike to his leg *(pahulog)*.

4th Principle – If your opponent is controlling your left hand, as soon as he abandons control of that hand, use it for an offensive strike. It was my compadre, Joe Villasin, who enlightened me in this method of utilizing immediately the newly-freed left hand to strike with, instead of leaving it where it is or for a block support. Again, like our slogan says, "It's all in the left hand."

Break the Feel

In close combat fighting, as your arms and hands get in contact, the sensitivity *(feel)* is immediately established. You have to keep contact with and be sensitive to the opponent's weapon and moves. If you want to go on the attack, break the "feel" and lose contact by lifting or breaking from the contact area so as to lose the opponent's sensitivity to your move. Strike wherever the opportunity presents itself.

Control and Capture the Opponent's Stick

Whether doing a defensive or offensive move, your left hand must be in ready position to capture your opponent's stick or defend against a counter-strike. Thus, the left hand must follow both the strike and the defense, at all times. Capturing will start with a cupping habit for workouts, and hooking for implementation, and should progress to wrist and arm control. This slows down the opponent tremendously. This could be demonstrated during lessons. It is one of the secrets of control. That is the essence of our motto: "It's all in the Left Hand." Control may come in the form of a subtle hook to slow down, or better still with a wrist hook and lock, which severely slows down response or subjects your opponent to control.

Iyahay — Grabbing the Lead

Iyahay is concept of leading the fight through left hand control and knowing where and how to shift the direction of your strike. You should also know advanced footwork, which is taking the steps to throw the opponent's timing off, shift his balance off or close the gap for a more effective and favorable strike. With this comes body flexibility, control of balance and timing. Finally, the thrust starts your control of the fight. This paragraph sounds coded. It is! Control the fight. This is now in the stage of *iyahay* or advanced fighting.

Anciong Bacon said that when you have attained a certain level of training where you no longer are led or subject to the lead of you instructor, you are said to be doing the *iyahay*. Roughly translated, this means "to each his own," although Jose Villasin called it "grabbing the lead." This skill emanates from understanding how to control the fight. Again, it all emanates from the left hand controlling the opponent's stick and then taking the lead. When you see demonstrations on YouTube, you are quickly impressed with the speed and variety of strikes. Unknown to the observer, it is the lead or the instructor that dictates the tempo, speed and variety of strokes and techniques. The students look only as good as what the instructor or master can dish out. When a person has reached this level, then he can apply the *kwentada* method of advanced planning by devising a plan of action using ruses and ploys to prompt a response. Based on the response, he can apply an unexpected strike or offensive move.

Simultaneous Attack & Defense

Avoid the common "one-two" mentality, i.e., defending first before delivering an offensive move. For Balintawak fighters, whenever possible, apply offensive strikes simultaneously with your defensive moves. This confuses, rattles and discombobulates an opponent. He would not know where the strike is coming from or how to respond or react to it.

Deliver simultaneous strikes with your block or defense as explained earlier. This is a signature of the Buot Ball Concept. It is difficult to predict, defend and counter. As opponent delivers his counter-strike, block with one hand and feel for an opening. If the blocking hand is open and not controlling your hand, use the same hand to attack. Use opponent's own inertia, momentum or force to deliver your strike.

Semi-Offensive, Half-Timing Strikes

The basis of semi-offensive strikes originates from the half-timing, broken cadence, rhythm or off-beat sneak strikes or side blows. For lack of a better word, Jose Villasin coined the term "half-timing" to indicate that response was done in split-time. As your opponent abandons control of your stick or hand to clear your left hand, control his stick before he can deliver a counter-strike and use the split second time to deliver an offensive move. It has been called "half-timing" as a means of gaining a split second advantage to take command of a situation, thus taking the lead by delivering an unexpected sneak strike. This is an offensive move that will not be anticipated by its insertion in between the normal counter strikes. These moves are inserted during play and not on first strike. Actually, it is a strike off the anticipated cadence or tempo of the strike.

Kwentada — Irregular and Unclassified Techniques

Kwentada is adapted from the Spanish word *cuenta,* which means "to count" or "calculate." (We spell it with a "K" since there is no "C" in the Filipino alphabet, which is also why we use the letter "K" in *Eskrima). Kwentada* is often used by eskrimadors without fully understanding the meaning and context of the word. It is a system of setting up, plotting, trickery, scheming and planning moves. In delivering a strike or a probing thrust, certain forced moves or logical counter-moves are anticipated from the opponent. If the opponent falls into this bait *(pa-on)* or trickery *(lansis)* of countering in the anticipated manner, then the set-up planned is executed. It is like split-second chess, applying both mastery of technique and split-second reflex. It is often claimed but rarely practiced or understood by most eskrimadors. More often than not, even Balintawak eskrimadors use the word but have no real clue as to its meaning and use. It just sounded sophisticated and mysterious. This was Anciong's and Villasin's secret. Here are four strategic methods for setting up an opponent to be struck by your real, intended blow.

1. Deliver a probing thrust either side, then *paapas*—i.e., do a fan blow to opponent's head to force him to block. When he does, control his hand and proceed to strike on the opposite side of his body.

2. *Paapas* twice, meaning, after doing a fan strike on one side of the opponent's head, shift your fan blow to the opposite side of his head. Control his hand and proceed to thrust or strike on the opposite side of opponent's body.

3. As the opponent pulls back (retracts) his stick to strike you *(berada),* strike him! This is our argument against pulling back the stick, which in the first place telegraphs your move and delays your timing.

4. As the opponent delivers a strike, bob or weave to avoid the strike. As the opponent's stick passes you, and shortly before it comes to a stop at the top of his strike, bridge and enter to deliver your strike.

This is knowledge I will not bring to my grave. I will share it. For lack of a better term, Jose Villasin has called these "offensive moves" as refinements of *kwentada*. The old man Bacon just did and executed the technique without naming it or even calling attention to it. He taught it to his students but to those less observant, unless it was clearly pointed out, the student would go through the moves without knowing his capacity for better controlling of the fight. It is like the "fruit of knowledge" – "the fruit of good and evil." It is the ability to recognize what you know and to use your knowledge judiciously. The reason the grandmaster did not point it out was probably because it caused the trainee to be too difficult to handle. With little knowledge or worse yet, ignorance of the art, a student would go into offensive controls and that would make it difficult for the teacher to teach him or train him.

In Balintawak Eskrima, especially under Jose Villasin, the term "offensive stage" had a very special and significant meaning attached to it. Many Balintawak eskrimadors never knew nor understood it. Even students of Villasin who were never taught the technique thus never understood it. It was a mystery that Villasin protected so carefully. It kept him in control of the strong and young upstarts.

Offensive *kwentada* is the apex and summit of eskrima knowledge. It is the ability to always control a fight. The fighter who has achieved this stage of proficiency controls the timing, dictates the pace and chooses the strikes. It places the opponent on the defensive and keeps him busy reacting and countering the strikes rather than choosing his options and offensive moves.

Unknown to many instructors they are using the techniques to some degree but don't understand its mechanics. It is used in teaching students. Students are often not in the position nor do they have the knowledge to challenge or question the master. The student was always in submission to his superior. He was always the *inagak* instead of *nagagak or tigagak,* meaning he was always the student instead of teacher or leader. You find this in demonstrations of the *palakat,* even at full dazzling speed; the student is only responding to the strikes and never initiating the strikes.

In actual combat, there is no longer a student-teacher relationship but rather it is showdown and battle for dominance, control and conquest. This higher form of the art is called the *kwentada* method, often mouthed by Balintawak eskrimadors but hardly and very seldom understood and fathomed. Both fighters may apply the *kwentada* method. The fighter who can apply the so-called "advanced techniques" or has better reflexes of using his "advanced technique" wins, since he quickly forces his opponent to go on the defensive. I don't remember the grandmaster teaching these techniques of assertion in an explicit manner. If he did, it was couched in vague, obscure and ambiguous terms. He always claimed that he taught everything, which was in fact a truth. A student just had to be quick and observant to understand and comprehend it. By now, everything really sounds cryptic and mysterious. It is. That was the genius of Anciong Bacon. Jose Villasin was the man who deciphered the "Rosetta Stone" of Anciong's hieroglyphics. Those are my lost treasures.

Advanced Techniques

As a step up, the "advanced techniques" will further place the fighter in a controlling situation. Villasin called this "grabbing the lead." Anciong and Teddy used the term *iyahay*, meaning "to each his own." It is a technique he did not openly teach to the chagrin of many of his students. One of the techniques is that after delivering a probing strike, always cross to take the lead, then control the opponent's stick to break his timing. It is from this point that the master proceeds to dictate the fight. The split second hesitation by the opponent gives you the authority to dictate the timing of the play. Then thrust: the opponent is then set to your pace of timing. He is now on the defense. He is just reacting and responding to the give and take of the fight. Still cryptic. Remember, you heard it first here.

For the advanced player, unpredictability and speed in execution are the keys. The less your opponent is able to predict your move, the more you have the upper hand. The quicker you react—i.e., before he can respond or figure out your next move—the better your chances are of executing your offensive moves. Then of course other factors such as mastery of superior techniques, confidence, courage, power and strength come into play.

It used to baffle Anciong's students how he would choose his target and predict where it would land. I tried to share this knowledge earlier with some of my colleagues but they ignored, flouted and snubbed my offer. They thought I was just full of it. At my age now, I cannot carry this knowledge to my grave. Even Villasin died without sharing this knowledge to almost all of his students. "Advanced" training was such a mystery at the club that I became a pariah as a possessor of this secret knowledge. I even witnessed a student weep, begging Villasin to teach him "offensive stage" fighting. Many great fighters use and apply it but do not understand its application and they even deny its existence. Even Anciong and Teddy Buot denied its existence, although they used it. Both Teddy and Anciong used the term *iyahay.*

Its application momentarily baffles and confuses the opponent, loses time and tempo and places him on the defensive. There were other advanced techniques that were so secretive, that I refused to write them down for fear others would find out about it. I forgot the details of their execution. Unfortunately, disuse leads to forgetfulness, what I call selfish stupidity – forgetting where you hide your treasure is just lunacy. Has this ever happened to you? Anyway, many hidden treasures have been lost forever by its owner and keeper. Those were my lost treasure.

When an opponent applies any attack techniques, *apply semi-offensive and counter-offensive techniques* immediately, such as: butting; side blows; disarming or take away; kicking; tripping and sweeping; boxing blows; slipping, bobbing and weaving; elbowing; breaking balance; pushing and pulling; step on; kneeing; leg swings; takedowns and throws; holds; arm-bars; etc. After control:

1. Immediately re-assert offensive by initially delivering a thrust to regain control, to take the offensive move and apply options.

2. Apply advanced stepping techniques, e.g., stepping forward and left or forward and right and proceeding to control.

3. Apply advanced techniques to groups.

Master Your Art

First of all, you should have superior knowledge and skills to your art. Meaning, you must have a wide variety of options and moves. You must have the basic perfection of form and delivery and mastery of your art. You must have the quick reflexive skills to summon your knowledge without groping or searching for a response. In moments of extreme fear or excitement, the heart rate goes extremely fast and the brain freezes, the muscles freeze and only instinct and reflexes take over. Reflex comes only from correct repetitive practice.

Deciding What's at Stake

Decide what is at stake. Is it a fight which demands brutal and deadly retaliation or is it just one that merely means keeping the opponent subdued and under control through submission holds or perhaps disabling techniques or even deadly force?

Martial art is taught as a privilege to responsible individuals and not to trouble seekers. It could be deadly and thus should be handled prudently realizing legal and moral consequences. Self-defense is just that, *defense* of one's self, his family and maybe strangers. Besides, a person with hurt pride or full of embarrassment because of unreasonable use of superior strength could plot revenge and even murder. A person who realizes that he had it coming to him will likely accept his beating as a deserved comeuppance for his own stupidity and irrationality. Avoid shame as this could lead to vengeance and treachery. Counter-offensive moves are for confrontations calling for self-preservation.

Handle Psychological Distress

Martial artist who practice self-defense techniques daily, should react in a reflexive and spontaneous manner even in extreme stress and fear. Even for the trained fighter, anger or surprise may cause uncalled for reactions. Eskrima emphasizes close combat training and tries to impart presence of mind in life or death situations, when you have to defend your life or those of your loved ones. In situations like this, panic sets in – the heart beat races beyond the normal rate of 80-112 beats per minute to a staggering 145 or more beats per minute, there is shortness of breath, dry mouth, trembling, the muscles freeze, there is auditory exclusion, you cannot hear, gross motor skills decrease and all fine motor skills are lost as the brain freezes. It is the basic fight or flight for survival response. The best martial artists function best under these circumstances.

This is when only the large muscle groups can be summoned. Instinct, reflexes and training take over or should take over. The brain no longer functions, but only spontaneously reacts. The question then is, can we summon our reflexes from our training? That can only be answered when the situation presents itself. As I have earlier said, "you will only be as good as your worst self during daily workouts. Train like you are in a fight and fight as you have trained." When the adrenaline pumps, be sure your reflexive response will answer the call of the situation. As someone said, and as I have said elsewhere, you will only be as good as your worse day of training.

The Warrior Mentality

Courage, mental and fanatical resolve to win are usually the edge that wins any game or fight. It is true in the Olympics or any other sporting event. It is true with the kamikaze fighters and the suicide bombers. Besides, even the look of anger, rage or even a stare of confidence can unnerve an opponent. With this comes the "killer instinct" of winning. This is the winning edge of any competition. Watch fighters before a fight, witness primal cries of football players or karateka.

Those are shouts to instill fear or to boost their own confidence. It is the psychological edge; the will to win wins fights and competitions.

Legal Consequences

From my experience as a Philippine lawyer, I know that in the event of litigation, the odds will be against you as a trained martial artist. Your fists and superior strength and knowledge are considered aggravating circumstances and deadly weapons and will be used against you. Your claim of self-defense better be solid and without holes. If there is a crowd gathered, raise your hands (this is an offensive position by the way) and say out loud, "I don't want a fight." Witnesses have to see and hear that you did not start the fight and that you backed off and declared your plea for avoiding a fight. You have to "jury proof" yourself. If the inevitable happens, do not talk to the cops or anyone and try to justify yourself. The Miranda Rights gives you the right to remain silent otherwise what you will say will be used against you in court, and it will. Remember, you acted "to stop the threat to you, your family and a stranger" and do not even say, "I did it in self-defense." That is a legal conclusion.

CHAPTER 11

ASSORTED INDEPENDENT TECHNIQUES

These are some of our "go to" techniques that we apply for time to time. We try to vary our moves to interest our students and to confound our foe. We also try to record some of our earlier methods and procedures. The techniques mutate from teacher to teacher, the way we learned it or understood it. Some have purposely modified it or improved on it through the years. We also use Cebuano terms and try to familiarize our worldwide audience to the vocabulary of every day eskrimadors the Philippines. In gratitude, I have given credit or reference to the people I saw it first or learned it from. In the final print due to some editing and the reduction of the text, the credit I have given may not appear. My apologies if this happens.

1. *Sapwang/Juego Todo* - Grab, Swing and Full Strike

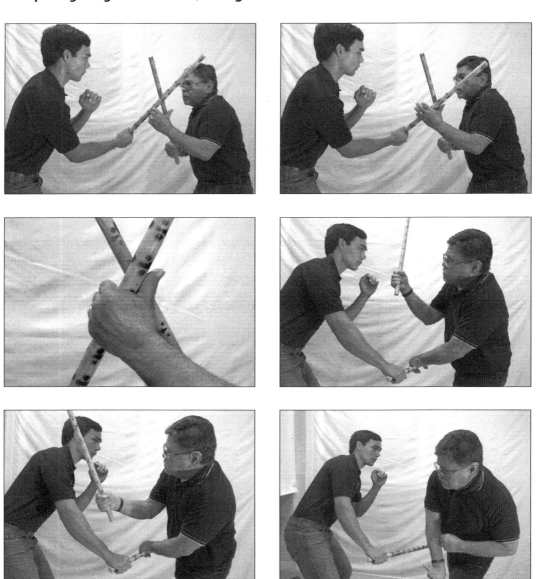

As sticks are crossed on your left side, swing over both his and your stick, palm up, from your left side to your right side. Grab both sticks, palm up, and flip them to your right side. With full force, deliver a power strike to the left side of the opponent's head or face.

2. *Tukas* – To Open Up, Uncover or Unveil

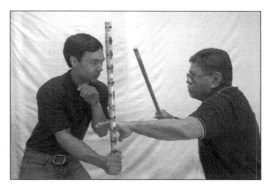

As the sticks cross in blocking a strike number 1, insert your left hand in between the X. Shift your hand from the back hand by turning your thumb down. Push his weapon hand and stick to your left to open up for a strike and deliver a simultaneous number 1 strike to the left side of oppnent's head.

3. Abaniko – aka Pa-Apas, Witik, Redondo, Paypay

This is a basic fanning, or switching hit, from one side to the other by means of a quick wrist snap action. The photos show simple example, here is how to use it from a number 1 or 3 strike, control palm down and *abaniko*. Strike a fan strike to his left. As opponent chases then a fan strike to his right sending your opponent chasing your stick, and strike another fan strike to his left, follow with a power strike on is right.

4. *Pokpok/Puño* – Butting to Opponent's Face

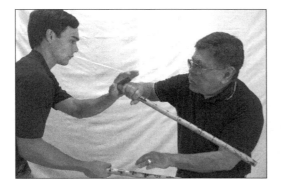
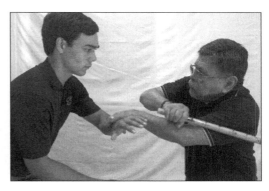

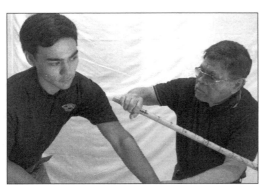

After inside cross to block, grab opponent's right wrist from under the crossed sticks and jerk hard to your left and then butt strike the opponent's face.

5. Supo/Pokpok – Blunt Butting to Opponent's Hand

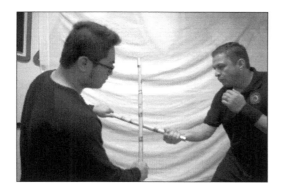 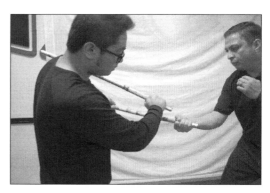

This technique is a concept based on a two-step action of blocking the opponent's strike and countering immediately with a strike to his weapon hand with the *puño*, or butt end of your stick. I have shown several examples here.

continued

5. Supo/Pokpok... continued

 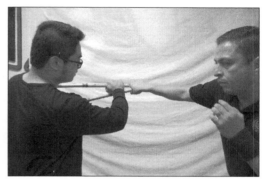

6. Finger Clip

After a block a strike to your right side (i.e., 2, 3 or 6), and if opponent has a long grip, snake the tip of your stick under his arm. Grip your stick and the *puño* of his stick and squeeze to cause extreme pain. Alternately, if his grip is short, squeeze close to his grip for extreme pain.

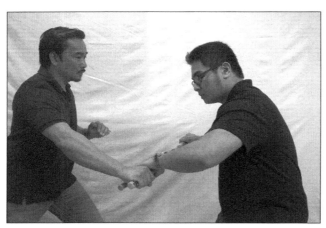

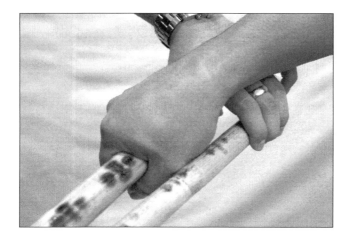

7. Neck Crank

 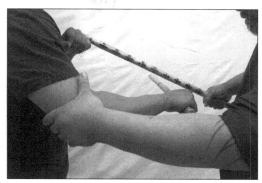

From a number 2 strike, block with your left hand and control is fist. Shift control to his left elbow and push to your right. Push your stick around the back of his neck, right around the carotid area, step left and push his shoulder to your right. Lower your head and push it against his neck and head leaving no space for him to counter and catch the end of your own stick. Grab, pull down, and crank as if revving a motorcycle. To induce extreme pain or cause a black out or worse. Warning, this is extremely dangerous and can cause death if the stick is directly on the carotid artery as it could cause blockage of blood flow to the brain or very serious injury or death.

8. *Kagis Ug Tabas* - Bruise, Scrape and Slash

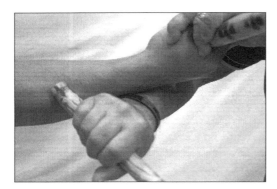

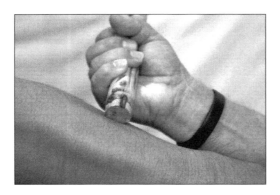

Instead of butting, scratch or scrape his arm with the butt of your stick or hit his forearm with your right hand. This is a nasty trick when applied during "friendly" workouts. You will go home with burning bruises not knowing how you got them. It is not life threatening, use this nasty trick.

9. S-Strike

After blocking number 1 strike, lift and transfer his weapon hand and stick with your left hand, palm up (with your left hand between the crossing sticks and his grip), to your right. Deliver a simultaneous "S" Strike (i.e., a left to right strike to the right side of opponent's head, right elbow or arm).

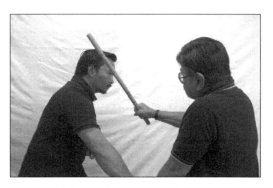

From strike number 2, your left hand controls opponent's stick as you shift the counter-strike from opponent's left to his right side in an "S" Strike or reverse number 1 strike (i.e., hitting the right side of his head instead of the left side).

10. *Palipat/Lansis* - Feinting and Ruses

Block a number 2 or 3 strike, then feint a strike to opponent's leg then suddenly shift your strike to his head.

continued

10. *Palipat/Lansis... continued*

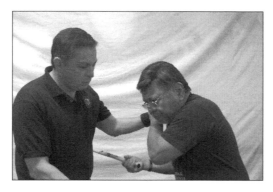 

Upon contact of sticks, slide your stick down on opponent's hand. Feint a strike to the left side of his head, control opponent's hand and shift the strike to his right side. Address strike to the left side of opponent's head and with wrist control and *witik* style; hit the right side of his head.

11. Snapping Fulcrum Strike and Control

After cross of sticks from block, use a snapping fulcrum maneuver by jerking down the opponent's stick with a simultaneous snapping strike.

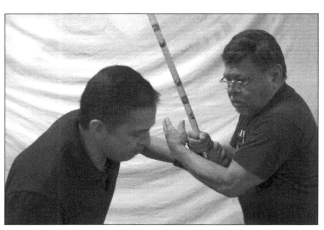

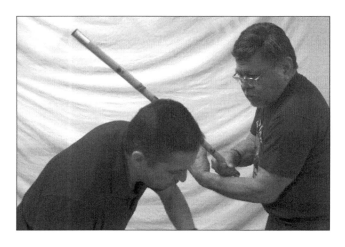

12. *Badlong* - Clear Check and Strike

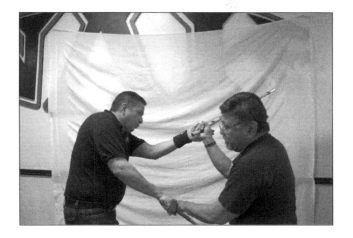

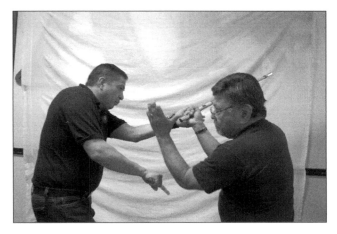

In delivering strike numbers 1 or 12, and if the opponent parries the strike over his head, slap his hand down with your left hand down with your left hand and proceed with your strike to opponent's head.

Badlong is often used as bait and as a *kwentada* technique or ruse and it is known as the "scolding hand" (*badlong*) based on Group I exercises of Lifting and Clearing. This is a very useful *Balintawak Eskrima* technique that may be used especially in knife fighting and other bare hand techniques. This is only a part of the ridiculed *tapi-tapi* system championed by Anciong Bacon that is now extensively copied by former critics and detractors. This also emphasizes the importance of the left hand in the fight. Again, this is the reason Anciong rejected the two stick system. Remember our motto: "It's all in the left hand."

13. *Corto* – Shortened Strike from Long Range *(Largo Mano)*

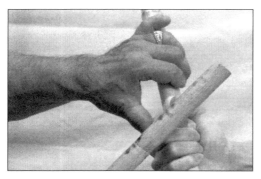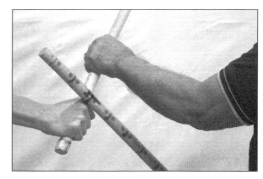

Corto Forehand   *Corto Backhand*

In long distance fighting, after initial cross to block the opponent's number 1 strike, step left and forward. Shift your weight left and strike the opponent's wrist or hand in a left to right slashing manner. Then strike again in a left to right strike and rush in to control and make further offensive moves.

Some styles call this method *largo mano,* Spanish for long hand. For some reason Balintawak (Villasin) has used the opposite term *corto,* meaning to shorten, probably meaning to shorten the long distance by this abbreviated or truncated strike to the hand or wrist, usually when the hand is unnecessarily extended making it an easy target.

14. *Labnot* - Jerk Down and Strike

Opponent delivers a number 1 or 4 strike, cross to block and grab his wrist. Jerk down and left with a simultaneous weight shift to your left and face obliquely left. Deliver number 2 strike.

If Opponent delivers a number 2 strike, block and immediately grip his wrist. Transfer your weight to your right foot and back and jerk back to your right and strike. Or twist and face right and do an S-strike to the right side of his head.

15. *Unay* – To Be Hit With Your Own Weapon

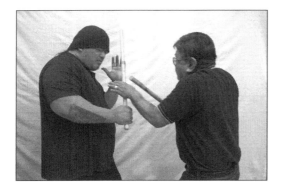 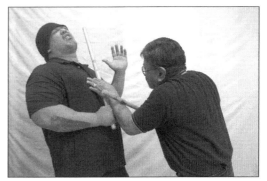

Upon blocking a number 2 or 3 strike, hold the opponent's stick and snap it on his own face. He will not anticipate the trick.

16. Instant Destruction

From a number 2 or 3 strike, block and take control. Open up by pushing his weapon hand to your left while simultaneously striking.

17. Wrist Curl

 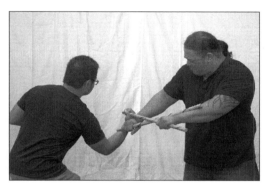

From a number 2 or 3 strike slip the tip of your stick over his stick and under his arm. Grab the tip of your stick, palm down, and push down both your hands towards his arm. This will be very painful and keep him locked for control. If you want to disarm, simply curl down both wrists as if revving up a motorcycle.

18. Shoulder Grab

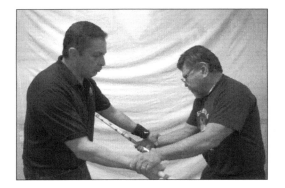 

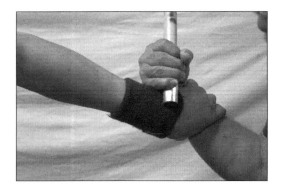 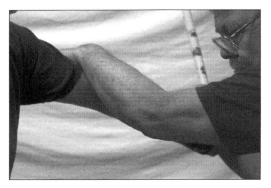

As the opponent grabs your hand and tries to control your stick, hook the butt of your stick around his grip to take back control. Grab under his armpit and jerk him to your left side and strike.

19. *Kabya* - Throwing Opponent's Hand Down

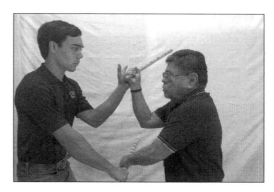

After blocking a number 1 or 3 strike, swing both sticks close to the grip and do an S-strike. You can also execute a number 1 or 3 strike.

20. Drill - Bobbing and Weaving with Sticks

 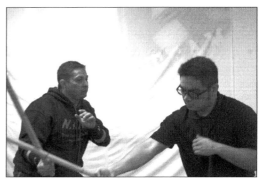

Student strikes a number 2 strike and instructor blocks; Instructor strikes student's head as student bobs; Student controls and counters with a number 1 strike; Student bobs and parries down instructors stick and strikes a number 1 strike; Teacher captures, controls and parries down; Instructor controls and strikes a number 2 strike; Student bobs; Student strikes a number 1 strike; Instructor blocks and controls; Instructor blocks, controls and delivers a number 2 strike; Instructor strikes a number 1 strike that student ducks, weaves and parries over; Student strikes a number 1 strike that instructor blocks to close. Repeat.

continued

20. Drill... *continued*

continued

20. Drill... *continued*

PART 5

BALINTAWAK INTERPRETED: APPLICATION OF BALINTAWAK

CHAPTER 12
DISARMING TECHNIQUES

We have over 70 disarms, also called snatching and take-away techniques. About half of them are shown here. For the purposes of illustration we have shown only a few basic disarms. I have ordered the disarms illustrated here as they are taught, and placed them into sections based on left or right side attacks. Further, it should be noted that there are counters for every disarm or move. For every offensive strike, there is a counter. General principles of countering are described here. With the examples given, you should be able to construct the other disarms with some thought and practice.

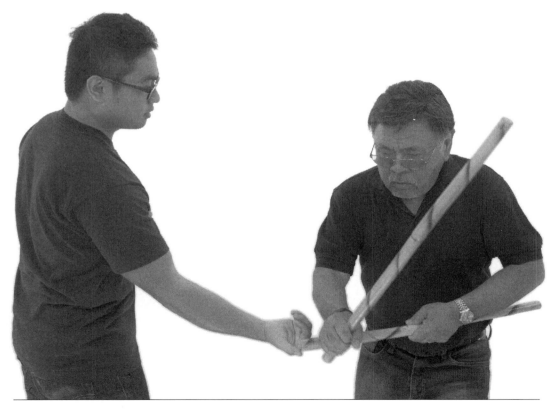

Disarms of Strikes to Your Left Side
(Numbers 1 & 4 Strikes & Number 7 Thrust)

1. Push Out, Basic - Balintawak Disarm Number 1

As opponent strikes to your left with a number 1 or 4 strike, do a standard defensive cross block. Capture and hold his stick with your left hand outside the cross, palm down. Twist his stick up with your thumb by pushing the butt of his stick upward in a counter-clockwise movement. Snap his fist down with your right fist or your right forearm to disarm the stick. In real combat, hit his grip with the butt of your stick as you snap down to disarm.

2. Bang Down - Mike's Modified Disarm

 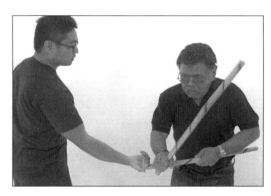

After the basic block, push his stick up with your left hand as you twist it to make the butt of his stick point upward. Bang down with your right forearm onto his grip, or palm heel to disarm as you pull with your left hand while twisting counter-clockwise.

3. Bang Up Disarm

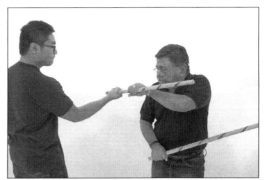

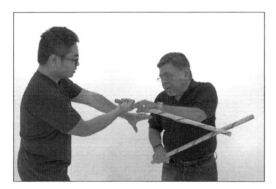

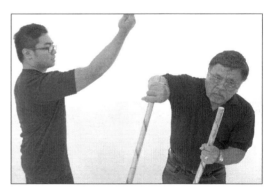

As a number 1 or 4 strike comes, cross the sticks to block and gain inside control with your left hand. Slide your grip under his grip, then bang up with the back of your wrist or with your forearm to disarm the weapon as you twist to your left.

4. Push Across Scissors – Bobby Taboada's Variation

As a number 1 or 4 strike comes, cross with outside control and grab the opponent's stick. Twist his stick counter-clockwise while pushing the butt of his stick upward. Push the stick with both hands in an X-position toward his right shoulder to disarm the stick.

5. *Corto* and Flip Under

As a number 1 or 4 strike comes, cross with inside control. Control his wrist with your left palm up and lay your own grip close to his hand. Push down with your left hand and pull with your right hand to strip and disarm. Note: If you want to make the stick fly, flick farther out. If your push down, watch for your foot, step back with your right.

6. *Corto* and Flip Under II - Frank's Accidental Variation

This is a variation on the above disarm. Instead of striking, slip your stick (tip first) under the opponent's stick to lay your stick on his arm and stick close to his grip. To make the move effective, push his stick with your left hand to your right hand and lay your stick palm-up to make the crossing sticks more of an X-shape for better leverage. Flip his stick down and under to disarm.

7. One Hand Crank Disarm - Showboating by Bobby

From number 7 thrust, take control from outside the cross. Hook the butt of your stick under the opponent's stick resting the butt of your stick on his arm. Quickly withdraw your right hand as you release your stick and, using your own stick as a fulcrum, pull down on the opponent's stick with your left hand as it applies pressure on his grip and on his arm to disarm.

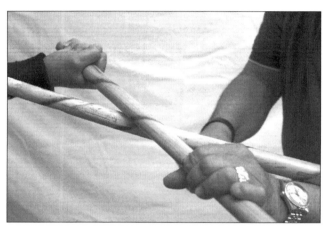

8. Snake - Common Eskrima Disarm

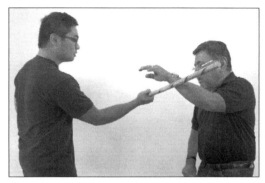 

 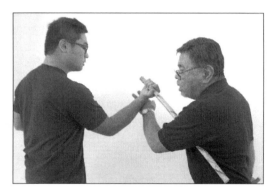

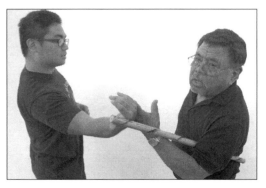

After a defensive block on your left, snake your left hand on top the cross and under his grip in a counter-clockwise movement. Pull to your left and back to disarm.

9. Clip on Chest - A Standard Number 7 – Villasin Style

From a number 7 thrust, block and slip your left hand under the opponent's stick. Control his grip and pull it towards your chest. Turn to your right and bend down, making sure to compromise his grip to disarm.

10. Clip On Chest with Bang Up Strip – Ryan Buot's Variation

After blocking a number 7 strike, lay your stick close to the opponent's grip and close to your chest. With your left hand palm up close to his grip, and your right grip close to and on top of his wrist, jerk up with your left hand. Simultaneously jerk down with your right grip at a point close to his grip to strip way the stick.

11. Goose Neck - Top Strong Arm and Reverse to Disarm

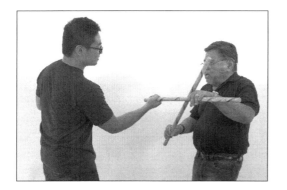 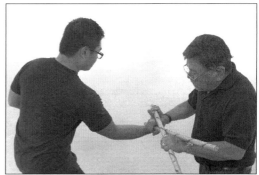

 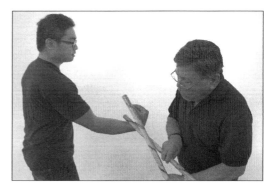

 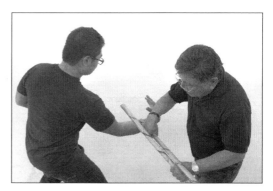

This is a good disarm if your opponent is strong and tries to muscle you. After a 1 or 3 strike, block and take outside control on your left by holding his stick. Slide the butt of your stick under his grip, then snake the butt on your stick on top his grip. Pull and jerk down to your right with the butt of your stick with a body twist and weight shift to your right. Reverse direction with the butt of your stick on top and push his grip to the left with your fist or right forearm to disarm. If he resists, repeat the procedure.

12. Anciong's Number 5 Strip

Parry the number 5 thrust. Control the opponent's stick with your left hand. Hit his grip with your fist (in real combat, hit with the butt of your stick). Simultaneously pull and jerk your left hand to effect the strip disarm.

13. Anciong's Number 5 Strip – Alternative

Block the number 5 thrust. Control the opponent's wrist with your left hand. Strike his hand with the butt end of your stick in real combat or push his grip with your fist close to his grip. Pull and jerk with your left hand as you simultaneously push with your right hand to strip away the weapon.

14. Wrist Flip Under Strip

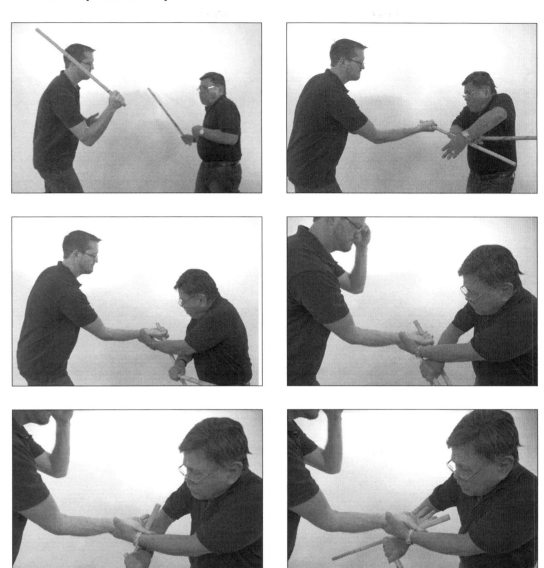

Block a number 1 or 4 strike, and with your right wrist on top his stick close to the wrist and your left hand on his wrist, do a wrist flip under. Pull with your left hand and push with your right to your right to disarm.

15. Delfin Lopez's Grandstand Pullout

This is Bobby Taboada's showboating favorite, used more for humor during demonstrations.

From a number 1 or 4 strike or a 7 thrust, block and hold the opponent's stick. Feign, threaten and simulate a strong thrust. Jerk your left hand to pull down as you simulate your thrust. For fun, toss your stick back to him to catch. He may be too startled to catch it. Laughter!

16. Sal's Side Strike Disarm

From a number 1 or 4 strike, block with the basic X-block. Take inside control his stick with your left hand and strike his right side with a slashing strike. Pry the opponent's arm and stick up as you push down with your left hand to control and lift your right grip up against his arm to disarm.

17. Long Grip Disarm

To discourage long grips, as the opponent strikes a number 1 strike block with the standard X-block. Grab the *puño* or grip of opponent's stick and pull it to your left as you use your own stick as leverage for the disarm.

18. Insert and Flick Under

From a number 1 or 4 strike, take control from the outside. Insert the tip of your stick over the opponent's arm and place your own stick on your left forearm. Pull your hand out and push down with your left hand to pry his grip loose and disarm.

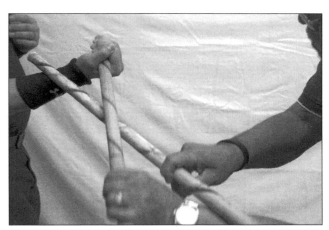

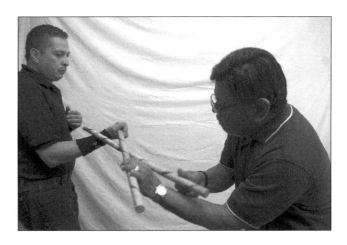

19. Single Stick Disarm

As the strike nears, step forward right and block the opponent's hand palm down with both of your hands. Controls the opponent's stick with your left hand while your right hand covers his grip. Push opponent's grip up with your right hand and push his stick down with your left hand to disarm. Note: You can use the same defense with a baseball bat strike.

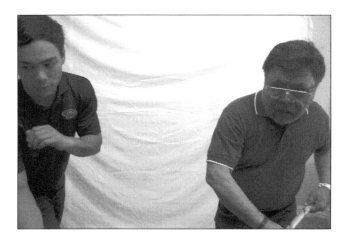

Disarms of Strikes to Your Right Side
(Numbers 2 & 3 Strikes and Number 6 Thrust)

20. Balintawak Snatch II

Defend a number 2 or 3 strike to your right by doing a right inside block with the tip of your stick pointing up. Slip your right wrist on top of opponent's weapon, close to his grip for better leverage. Reverse control of your left hand under his right hand as a platform to support his wrist up, as you jerk his stick downward with your right forearm to disarm. Caution: Withdraw your left foot; otherwise his stick could stab your foot.

21. Anciong *Suyop* Disarm

The *suyop* movement is like absorbing the strike with an open left hand, as if catching a ball, palm facing down. This technique applies whether: 1) he instructor delivers an initial strike number 1 and student blocks and counter strikes with a number 2 or 3 strike. Instructor blocks with his palm heel to absorb the force of the strike and sucks and absorbs as a brake to the strike *(suyop)* toward his body. Instructor's stick in defensively under the opponent's stick. Instructor's grip is pointed up and the point of instructor's stick is pointed down. Instructor clips students stick to his chest by pulling his grip in. Instructor strikes under student's stick to student's head. Instructor clips student's stick to his chest with his right grip and controls student's stick palm up as a fulcrum for a disarm. Instructor hooks his right grip over student's stick and jerks down with his right as he props up the wrist with his left to disarm.

22. Sam's Safety Variation of Anciong's *Suyop* Disarm

This variation of Anciong's *suyop* disarm is safer because you block first. After a standard block slip your stick under opponent's stick in preparation for a strike. Clip his stick on your forearm and strike under his stick. Reverse your left hand, palm up and under his grip, as a fulcrum. Clip his stick on your chest with your left hand and strike. Transfer control of his stick to your right hand and reverse your right hand grip and slip it on top his stick and snap down to disarm.

23. Clip On Chest Disarm - Villasin style

After a probing thrust to your right side, or after you block a number 2 or 3 strike, slip the butt end of your stick under the opponent's grip to clip his stick between your forearm and your biceps. Bang his grip upward with your left hand (palm up) and twist to the right to disarm the weapon.

24. Nilo's Disarm

After doing an inside block on your right side, with palm down, grab the opponent's stick, reverse your left hand control, palm-up, and twist opponent's stick downward and clockwise and back to your left to disarm the weapon.

25. Thrust and Right Arm Snake Disarm

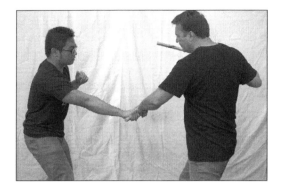 

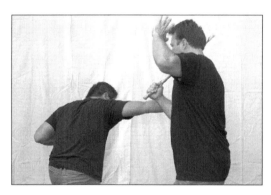 

From a number 2 or 3 strike, block with inside control. Control the opponent's stick from the outside with your left hand. Feign a thrust to his chest with your stick but instead snake the tip of your stick under his wrist and upward while controlling his hand with your open palm, placing his grip in a compromising position. Hit his arm or grip with your open left palm as you turn towards your right to disarm the weapon.

26. Left Arm Snake Disarm

Inside block his number 2 or 3 strike and snake your left hand over and under his grip as you pull down to disarm.

27. Villasin Clip on Shoulder (1) – Against Strikes 2 or 3

Defend against a number 2 or 3 strike with a standard X-block. Clip the opponent's stick to your right shoulder, palm down. Pull with your left hand towards your chest for control then push with your forearm or right shoulder to disarm the weapon.

28. Flick Down

Block a strike to your right side and take control by grabbing the opponent's stick, palm up. Push his grip down close to your grip. As you push your grip up, pull his stick down to disarm.

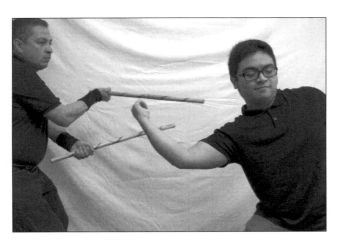

29. Snake and Crank

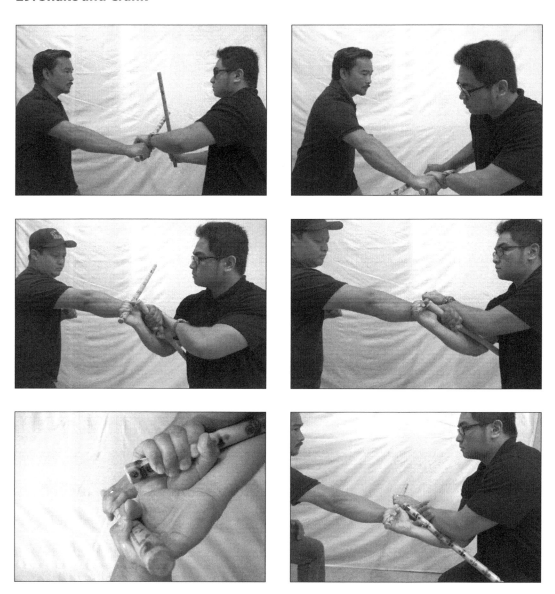

Block a number 2 or 3 strike. Threaten a thrust and insert your stick over his stick as in doing a *cabra*. Hook your stick over the opponent's stick, the tip of your stick now pointing right. Crank down as if revving a motor cycle, crossing over to inflict pain to aid in the disarm.

30. Clip on Chest Turn-Over

Block a number 2 or 3 strike then clip the opponent's stick under your armpit. Push opponent's hand up with your left hand to compromise his grip strength. Push down to your right to disarm the weapon.

31. Wrist Curl

 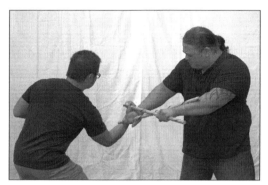

From a number 2 or 3 strike slip the tip of your stick over the opponent's stick and under his arm. Grab the tip of your stick, palm down, and push both of your hands down towards his arm. To disarm, curl down both wrists as if revving up a motorcycle.

Principles of Countering Disarms

- Lower your stick to change opponent's position. Be sure to maintain control by controlling his elbow.

- Slide your hand to place your wrist at an advantageous and stronger position.

- Bend your knees for greater stability.

- Do opposite to opponent's intentions.

- Break opponent's balance while maintaining your balance.

- Twist your grip counter-clockwise. If opponent has a very strong grip, loosen your grip to twist your control to be in a stronger position.

CHAPTER 13

BAREHAND TECHNIQUES

Barehand techniques are called for when we are not carrying weapons and so they are applied at close range. My immediate thought is to apply *simultaneous offense and defense*, which I teach to my students and which I call *counter-offensive moves*. To my knowledge, it is not traditional in other martial arts. Most apply a defense and offense mentality. I believe that can be improved. Some techniques in other arts seem to apply it without any effort to bring it to the conscious state. My effort is to bring our Eskrima to that level of consciousness. I observed Anciong apply the technique with sticks but he did not openly discuss it as a technique. Before jumping into our primary barehand concept and techniques, let us review the main striking points on the body. This is important for knowing where to strike as you learn how to strike.

Vital Striking Points

Warning: Some of these striking points may cause serious injury or death. Practice with caution

Strike on the Abdominal Area — When punching the abdomen, aim for the liver, spleen, solar plexus, kidneys and ribs.

Strike with a Head Butt — Head butt the mouth, nose, eyebrows and temple. Strike the coronal structure of the head (the soft spot on the baby's head). Strike behind the earlobes where the skull meets the neck.

Strike the Temples — Strike with both hands simultaneously on the front and side region of the head with a heavy handed and deep hitting technique. This causes disorientation. The jarring of the brain in the cranium and stop of blood flow by hitting the temporal arteries can cause a knockout. Striking the temple, the jaw below the ear, or the lower jaw can also cause a knockout.

Strike the Carotid Arteries — Striking the carotid arteries will stop blood flow and cause a knockout. Cutting the blood flow by choking the carotid arties can cause serious injury or death.

Strike Head/Face Vital Points — Strike the eyes, nose, mouth, lower jaw, Adam's apple (larynx) and the base of the throat.

Strike the Upper Back — Strike that raised ridge on the upper back with a downward elbow strike.

Strike the Tailbone (Coccyx) — Strike the tailbone (coccyx) with a kick or hand technique.

Strike Pectoral Muscles — Hit that floating rib just below the chest with your knuckles down and out.

Strike with an Open Palm — Block the number 1 strike or punch with an open palm strike on the hollow between the forearm and the bicep followed by an open palm slap behind his right ear followed by one on his left ear.

Strike the Triceps — Strike under the triceps, slipping and hitting inside the arm under the triceps.

Strike the Outer Thigh — In close combat, strike the outer thigh with a kick, knee or hand.

Kick the Leg — Follow with a strike to the jaw for a knockout.

Hit the Floating Ribs and kidney — Follow up to the jaw for a knockout.

Strike the Brachial Plexus and Neck Region — These are the areas both above and below the collar bone. This is only informational. It is a very dangerous area to strike. Poke the base of the throat. Strike the muscles at the base of the neck.

Strike the Leg — Hit the inner thigh or outer thigh, especially from a sitting position. Also hit the inner or outer leg. Thump on the foot bones, the tarsals and metatarsals.

Strike the Back of the Neck — Strike the third vertebrae, halfway between the base of the head and the shoulder.

Strike the Solar Plexus — Strike up into that triangular area at the intersection where the floating ribs meet. Also strike above the pubic bone but below the navel.

Strike the Groin — This is of common knowledge. Also grab the groin and squeeze.

Strike the Liver and Spleen — Strike the unprotected area below the floating ribs. Most boxers would choose to hit this area.

Grab the Love Handles — Pinch and grab some flesh on the love handles or underarm above triceps. This causes pain.

Hook a Punch — As you parry over with your left simultaneously from underneath hook your right hand to capture his wrist and jerk down to break his balance

Padungan **Concept**
Simultaneous Counter Offensive

In Cebuano, the terms should be *padungan* – the simultaneous delivery of a block or defensive move with an offensive move or strike. We may call it a *simultaneous offensive counterstrike*. As your opponent delivers a strike or counterstrike, block with one hand and feel for the direct opening to the opponent's body. If the blocking hand has the opening and opportunity to strike, strike with the blocking hand. Use his inertia, force or momentum to deliver the strike then deliver your counterstrike. The counter strike could be with your feet, knee, elbow or head. You can execute a simultaneous snap kick, leg swing, and knee to the groin, finger thrust to the eye or throat. The counter strike may be two counter strikes such as a simultaneous strike and snap kick. You can be assured your opponent will be stunned and shocked. You may also call it "shock and awe," to borrow General Arnold Schwarzkopf's famous phrase.

To obtain power and a knockout punch, swivel your body and hit through the target about three inches and snapback (like snapping back a wet towel). Hitting deeper will simply be pushing. The four important elements are: distraction, surprise, accuracy and power. Then you may finish with another technique if he isn't yet ended.

Parries

Part of what makes the *padungan* effective is the use of parries. In Balintawak we use three basic types of parries, as briefly described here.

- Outside parry is when you parry from outside the line of attack. Slip the punch and move your head to the left.

- Inside parry is when you move inside the punch to parry and then apply a technique.

- Hook parry is when you do an outside parry and hook the punch to your left to open your opponent to an unexpected strike.

Now that we have looked at striking targets, considered the *simultaneous offensive counterstrike*, and understand the three types of parries, we'll next look at how they come together in assorted, individual techniques.

Assorted, Individual Techniques

1. Parry and Strike Against a Right Cross

Simultaneously apply a one-count counter-offensive, such as doing an inside block with a simultaneous hook on the opponent's arm to take control. Then strike his biceps and punch to his jaw.

2. Lock and Slam Down – Sam's Favorite Technique

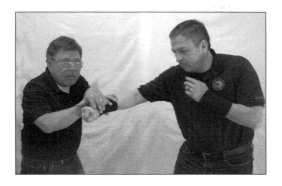 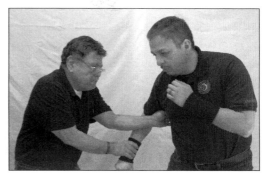

 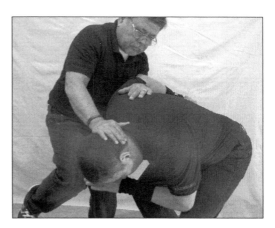

Parry down his right hand punch with your left hand. Slip your left hand under his armpit and hook it tightly behind his neck. Face slightly right as you grab the right side of his head with your left hand. (If he attempts to grab your leg, push his head. He cannot do it. Try it!) Control both his body and his head. Jerk his head down and simultaneously jam your knee into his face.

3. Balintawak Oldie I - Chicken Wing, Pull Down From on Top

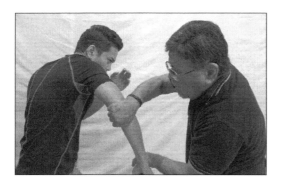 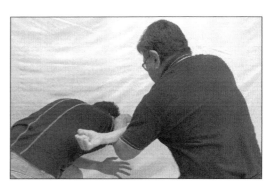

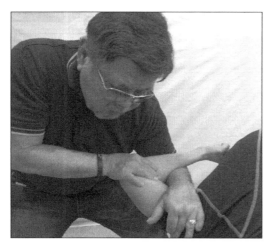

Parries over a number 1 or 4 strike and catch the top of the opponent's elbow and control his wrist downward. If opponent pulls his elbow up, push his wrist down. Control his arms with his left as he pushes down with his right on his elbow.

4. Balintawak Oldie II - Reverse Chicken Wing, Pull Down from Under

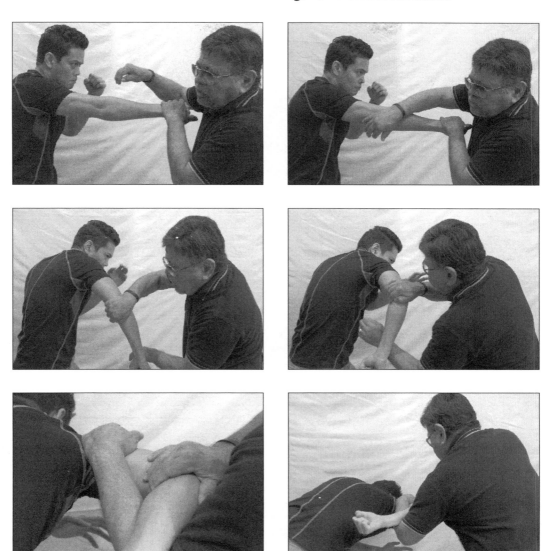

Block inside the punch with your left hand. Slip your right hand over the opponent's elbow, palm up, then pull up and then down. Reverse your left hand hold to raise and push opponent's wrist up. Increase pressure as you execute a "chicken wing" on him. He will try to reach your leg. Increased pressure will make it extremely painful and difficult to escape.

5. Knee Strike Counter Move

Parry the opponent's right punch with your left hand and strike his forearm with your right hand, either with a knife-hand on his arm or your knuckle on his forearm. Do a simultaneous knee strike to his leg.

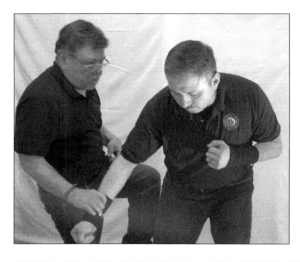

6. Parry and Kick

From a right cross, inside parry with your left hand to grab opponent's wrist with both hands while being ready to defend against his left hand. Grab opponent's wrist with your left hand, palm down, to pull as you and push his jaw with your right hand to keep him at bay. Do a round house kick to his thigh or jam his knee cap with a side kick or frontal kick while hanging on to his wrist for balance.

7. Palm Heel Strikes

Parry down or *paawas*. Jerk down with your left with a simultaneous palm heel the opponent's jaw or nose. With his right hand punch, block and simultaneously palm his chin, nose, mouth or finger thrust his eyes.

8. Web Hand Strike

As opponent punch with his right hand, block and simultaneously execute web hand strike to his throat.

9. Punch, Knee, Throw and Stomp

As opponent throws a right hand cross blocks with your left forearm and then slips his left under the striking hand and strikes his ribs. Parries opponent's hand down with your left hand and grab on top opponent's head as you slips your left arm under opponent's right arm to twist and flip him. Finish with a stomp, punch and drop down your left knee onto his ribs.

10. Big and Tall Takedown

 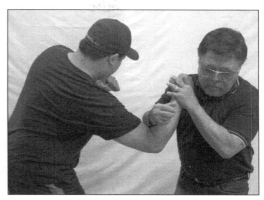

 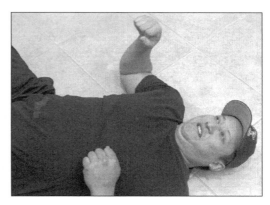

If grabbed on the shirt or if a punch is thrown, grab opponent's wrist with your left hand. Lay your forearm on opponent's forearm and step forward and left. Place your weight on opponent's forearm, control his left arm and suddenly jerk down. For better control, bend wrist inward to assure the fall.

11. Distraction with Takedown

 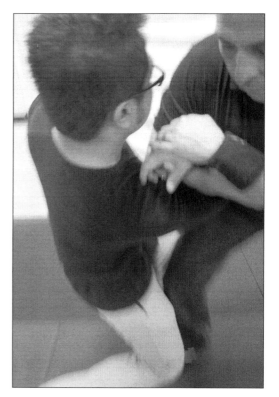

Before applying the previous technique, first do a frontal kick and then apply the takedown.

12. Side Choke

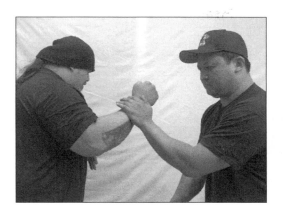

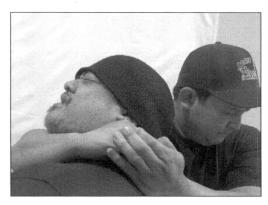

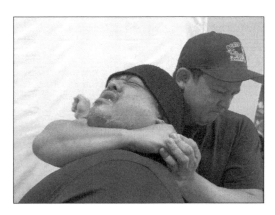

Parry opponent's right hand punch with your left hand. Step in front of his front right foot and push his shoulder to your right. Parry with your left and sneak your right arm under his arm with your right radical on his carotid artery and grasp your other hand and lock your grip. Push your head against his head to choke. Alternative: Grasp your left biceps and push his head with your left and lean back to choke.

13. Rear Choke

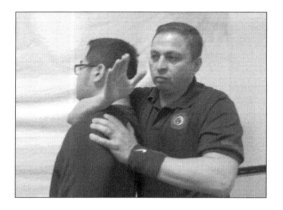 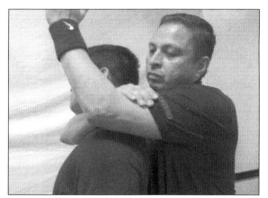

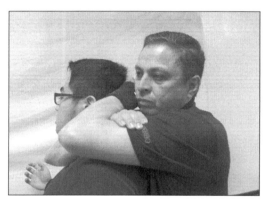 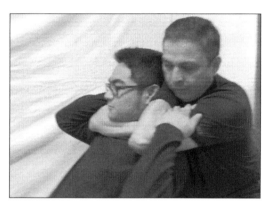

As opponent delivers a right hand punch or strike, slide your arm around opponent's neck with his carotid arteries resting on your biceps and your radial. Grasp your left biceps. Push down with your left hand on his head. Push your head against his head to place pressure on his carotid arteries and lean back to choke. Warning: This is very dangerous as person will pass out after 8-13 seconds and can cause death.

14. Single Leg Takedown from a Right Cross - Wally Jay Adaptation

Parry outside with your left hand and swing your right forearm above opponent's left knee and control his left foot down so that he cannot raise it. Pull his forward left foot along the floor in the direction of his foot as you push his thigh down to break his balance. Do not lift his right foot in doing your sweep as he will regain balance.

15. Arm Bar Against a Right Cross

Double parry the opponent's punch, grab his wrist and lay your radial on his triceps tendon (about an inch above his elbow) and grind it as you push him down.

16. Parry and Head Butt

From a right cross, outside parry with your right hand. Grab opponent's arm above the elbow and jerk it towards you, meeting his head, hitting his forehead or eyebrows.

17. Head Lock Control and Knee Strike

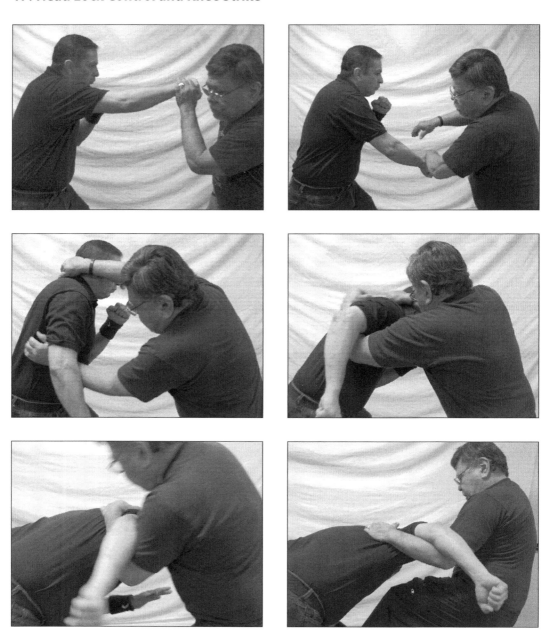

From a right cross, outside parry to your left. Parry down and grab the opponent's elbow from on top. Slip your left arm under his armpit and gab the nape of his neck. Push his head down while stabilizing your balance. Push his head down and away if he tried to reach for your leg. Knee him in the face.

18. Balintawak Drill

19. Punch Kick Drill

20. Boxing Drill

21. Bobbing and Weaving Drill

Advice for the Untrained

Allow me to teach you shortcuts to self-defense.

- Remember the theory of simultaneous defense and offense.

- Never strike with your fist unless you are a boxer. If you are untrained, you will break your wrist. Strike with your arm using your ulna which is your larger bone on your forearm to strike down on collar bone. Nothing fancy.

- Use your palm heel or knife hand to strike the mouth, nose, cheek, jaw, Adam's apple, neck or the gouge the eyes.

- Swing down on the groin. Most people know this. This is one of the most sensitive parts of a man, even a child's hit can hurt you.

- Use your knee to strike the groin or the inner and outer thigh.

- If you fall, grab a handful of sand and throw at his face.

- If grabbed - learn releases from holds, strike, scratch, scream, bite or spit if you must. Fighting is survival. It does not have to be pretty nor fair.

CHAPTER 14

DISCUSSION ON KNIFE FIGHTING

Knife fighting is a highly specialized skill and I will not pretend to be an expert in it. We do practice knife fighting and knife defense during workouts like all martial arts students do. The truth is, few teachers have ever been confronted with a bladed weapon or a gun. Most Filipinos do not have guns as they do in the west. Thus, the knife and blade culture have prevailed in the Philippines. It is cheap and available.

To start with knife fighting assumes both of the combatants have knives. Knife defense is shield against a knife attack. The term knife fighting is an oxymoron. The first principle and only principle is survival. Knife fighting is a matter of life and death. Are you committed to die or to kill? You do not win a knife fight; you survive it, if you are lucky. Will your pride compel you to stand your ground—either kill or be stabbed and slashed to death? There is hardly any middle ground. The situation is hardly planned. It usually is an attack or an assassination attempt. In a confrontation, one pulls a knife hoping that the threat will force the other party to back off and run. The other antagonist may also have a knife or he may not have a knife. The question now is fight or flight? If a person pulls a knife on you, would you even have the time to pull your own weapon?

Knowing how to stick fight does not necessarily mean you know how to knife fight. Further, the other person may have a gun. If you pull a knife on him, he will be justified to kill you. So don't be a smart ass. If the situation is such that you have been cornered, now what? If you freeze, you die. Regardless, those macho men who drive trucks with signs, *"NO FEAR,"* will surely pee in their pants or worse still, they will defecate in their pants.

Let me repeat, I have no experience in real knife confrontation and have no intention of trying my skills. We do train but it's all theory. So everything discussed here is based on theory and the assumption of perfect calm and presence of mind. Theoretically, the first thing a student of the martial arts should learn is mastery of techniques to the point of gaining reflexive action to any offensive move. Therefore, practice and better still, correct practice, is the beginning of mastery. As has been said, you are only as good as your worst day of training. In an actual fight, you will break into a cold sweat, your brain will freeze, you will lose your hearing, your jaws will lock and you will be unable to speak, your knees will turn to jelly, you will shake uncontrollably, your heart will race to 145 beats per minute, you will turn cold and your arms will turn to rubber and you will feel numb. Will muscle memory or reflexes take over?

Parrying should be reflexive. There should be no conscious thinking but rather reflexive reaction to any move. This works out with weapons or bare hand combat. Regardless of the angle of the attack or the hand in used quick reaction is of greatest importance. The next is to move out of the line of attack. These all seem like common sense decisions; but if a person does not have the correct reflexive move, he could move toward the weapon or worse still, fail to parry.

Use of bladed weapons is a large chunk of the Filipino fighting arts, it is a specialty and there are experts in this art and I acknowledge that there are those who claim to know it. The Philippines has a durable blade culture tracing back to prehistoric times. It was part of the attire of men to strap their blades to their waist and men felt naked without it on their side. The blade was what the six-shooter was to western cowboys. The stick has been made as a training tool in the drills and teachings the blade attack. However, there is a difference, the stick has no blade and it is not pointed. The stick has also been used to replace the blade as a striking and defense instrument. While the use of the blade, stick and even the empty hand moves and skills are consistent, they are not the same. In truth the bladed weapon is an assassin's tool. It may be used as a deterrent, threat, or means of intimidation. If the other person has a gun, as I said earlier, he could be justified in killing you for pulling a knife on him.

Knife fighting and defense was part of a different generation and a different culture. This is now the culture of guns that can be used at long ranges. It hardly needs skill to kill. So banish the thought that you will learn knife fighting and knife defense and walk with a swagger. You will be very dead. To start with, in the hands of a skilled wielder, a knife will be extremely difficult to defend against. The courts will also be unsympathetic to a knife wielder. In modern times, martial artists, police, law-enforcement officers and military men train in survival techniques in the use of bladed instruments. Many of the techniques are impractical in real life situations if you are not bent on killing. Thus for the most part the studies are academic in nature for a more practical understanding of the realities if and when confronted with a blade. Even qualified instructors seldom have combat or real life experience in blade fighting. Knife fighting should not be confused with knife defense when one of the combatants is unarmed. It is a survival skill only used in extremes. The legal repercussion in the use of knives and weapons are tremendous.

For academic discussion, there are so many varieties of knives whether spring loaded, throwing, folding, gravity, or fixed blade knives. For practical uses, the spring blades could malfunction and the folding knife could inflict injury on you. For practical usage, the balanced fixed blade knife without out fancy handle is probably best.

Never threaten with a knife unless you intend to use it in a life or death situation. You have secondary weapons aside from your hands and fists. You can use your elbows, knees, head, feet, teeth and legs at close quarters.

> *The only place where the knife fighting fantasy exists is in the martial arts. There is **no** such thing in the modern civilized world. In legal terms it is attempted murder, assault with a deadly weapon or homicide. To the street fighter it is assassination, not a "fight" at all. To the criminal it is a tool for robbery, rape or murder. Everyone else considers it repulsive and repugnant macho stupidity.*

PART 6

BALINTAWAK IN TRANSITION

CHAPTER 15

THE PHOENIX AND BUOT INFLUENCE

From my departure from the Philippines in 1978, eskrima has always been on my mind. Hardly anyone in Phoenix had even heard of Eskrima at that time. There were early pioneers like Remy Presas, who already had a book on Modern Arnis, naming himself as "The Father of Modern Arnis." There also were books by American author Bruce Tegner and some books by Irish, Swiss and German author's on cane fighting, but nothing like the eskrima we know. I bought these books, which I may have kept somewhere in my garage. These European books used the cane to hook the neck for self-defense, almost comical by eskrima standards. Remy's book was the closest I could see to the Eskrima I knew.

Sometime in the '70s, Jose Villasin and I scrutinized the stick or cane fighting books with rather critical and unflattering comments on what they offered. For this reason, Villasin visited Remy in his Manila studios. According to Villasin, Remy was rather coy and apologetic and said in his characteristic Ilonggo accent that he was doing this for the money. I am relating this from a historical perspective as a historian of Balintawak rather than as a dig on Remy. On the other hand I am very appreciative of Remy for his early effort in promoting arnis worldwide. He was serious and sincere in expanding his knowledge of the art. I suspect that this was when he started researching on Balintawak and searching out Anciong Bacon and ending up training with Arnulfo "Toto" Moncal, a student of Timor Maranga, who was one of the original members of Anciong's Balintawak in 1952. Remy searched out Teddy Buot and later Bobby Taboada as fellow Balintawak enthusiasts here in the US. Remy had since began incorporating Balintawak moves and identifying himself with Balintawak in his Modern Arnis style. Again, my brotherly kudos to the departed Remy, his students and his Modern Arnis; they are an integral part of arnis/eskrima history, and he is one of the worldwide powers in eskrima.

With the need for survival in a foreign country as an immigrant, eskrima was left in the cooler for a little while. Serendipitously, as a real estate investor and syndicator, with the collapse of the real estate market in the later '80s, I resumed my book writing that I started with Villasin in 1978. My book was first copyrighted in 1991 and I quickly published it on the Internet. Although it is copyrighted, it has been flagrantly quoted and rephrased by out-of-the-woodwork newcomers. This was when the world started hearing of the now legendary and fabled Anciong Bacon, Jose Villasin, Teofilo Velez, Teddy Buot and Bobby Taboada, all of whom I have lavished with praise. This much I claim as my part in spreading Balintawak

Eskrima worldwide. I am positive Teddy and Remy were in the meantime doing their part elsewhere in the US.

In Phoenix, I held classes in my backyard and in the backyard and *dojos* of my students, some of them owners of karate studios. There was nothing fancy about it. There was not one to challenge me with my skills; not with the stick anyway. Some of my students were serious martial artist who were eager to learn this exotic art, most of them black belts in their respective art. My sons never took me seriously, even to this day. I tried to impress them that this was a practical and indigenous Filipino fighting art worthy of Filipino pride. They were more into the high-kicking and flashy karate and tae kwon do.

There were no charges for my lessons. They were given out of love and as an evangelist and propagandist of the art. I was like John the Baptist crying out in the wilderness. There were few rewards but it was a passion that I possessed. There were few pictures and mementos to record my early attempts and I have forgotten the many names that have sporadically joined me. There were years of unrecorded memories—people, and events that have transpired—buried in the treasure chest of my remembrances. Only lately with the digital camera have we started taking a plethora of pictures. No films and printing to worry about!

Eskrima started with my sons kicking the bag and impressing their friends in the mid-80s. None of them stuck with it. As they say, "a prophet is not a prophet in his hometown." One of my son's friends, Adam Tompkins, was a skinny high school student who I don't even remember. From there on, he picked up martial arts and finally joined me a few years ago in eskrima. From my picture file, I can see that Craig Smith and Bart Vermilya were with me in 2003. That is over 10 years ago! Most of my students have left town for other cities and states, doing their thing and probably sailing the high seas of success elsewhere. Others have just abandoned eskrima as an impertinent part of their life.

FMA seminar and picnic at Papago Park -10-19- 2008

Balintawak Glendale with CNR, Mike Worden, David Buot, Danny Corpus, Sam Buot, Orville Turner, Orville's nephew, and Larry Vasquez, karate and kenpo school owner, circa 1984

Seminar at Chris Lopez Bobby, Willy and Chris Lopez

Orville & Nephew, 1984

Ryan with competition team gathering most medals

Orville, Nephew and Sam

Steve Dowd, Sam Buot and Craig Smith 6-7-2008

FMA Seminars at Margaret Hance Park 2010

Sam's Seminar at Margaret Hance Park 2011

Class at Sandovals 9-26-2003 with Craig Smith, Joe Staszo, Bart Vermilya, Sam, Allen Sandoval, Kim Essendrup and Don Hattery

Jon, Bart, Adam, Rob, Sam, Ryan, Bobby, Craig, Frank, Robert and Mike 11-10-2010

Adam Tompkins

Craig Roland Smith

Carlos Sevilla

Nick Thompson

FMA Picnic at Papago Park 3-29, 2009 - Ted Rabino, Sam Buot and John Jacobo

Sam and Craig at Philippine Independence Day Celebration 6-03-11

Sam, Bobby and George Bell on 9-30-2004

Bobby and Nick 11-13-10

Craig, Ryan, Sam, Nick, Bobby, Robert, Adam and Mike 11-13-2010

Balintawak Demonstration Team 10-24-10

Sam's 75th 3-19-11

Bob's mini-seminar at Chris Lopez' Brazilian JJ 10-19-2003

Bobby Taboada at home with Sam Buot, friends and students.

Pacquiao fight on 10-16-11

Eskrima group at Pacquiao fight 10-16-11

Weekly workouts at home on 9-22-10 with Ryan, Jon, Adam, Sam, Rob, Frank and Craig

Large, small and medium – Nick, Sam and Frank

FMA Picnic Seminar at Papago Park with Ted Rabino on 3-29-09

Sam's 74th birthday celebration 3-24-12

Seated (L to R): Thiel, Adam and Danny. Standing (L to R): Ryan, Sam, Chuck, Leonard, Mark, Bob and Carlos 10-28-11

Margaret Hance Park with Ted Rabino, Sam, Michael Butz and John Jacobo 10-31-11

Adam, Leonard, Bob, Chuck and Ryan 9-30-11

Greg Trent, Leonard Meuerer, Ryan Buot, Sam Buot, visiting Raul Tabili and Audie Betita

CHAPTER 16

THE FUTURE OF THE ART

We know not what is in store for the future of the art. Some styles in the United States have expanded the art to include MMA style fighting with full contact strikes with sticks. Yet, with all kinds of padding, it robs the art of its original essence of graceful stick fighting. Some have lost the art altogether with clumsy and awkward strikes. They beat each other senseless as if beating a mad dog with little to no technique at all, just plain wild strikes. Unprotected combat would obviously be too dangerous and would never find acceptance in litigation-prone USA. Waivers would have to be signed acknowledging the dangers that could result in serious injury of even death, like duels or the *bahad* of old. It is doubtful that the written agreement would even hold water in court. It would be considered *void ab ignitio* or void from the beginning since it would be considered an illegal contract. It will no longer be pure eskrima – just armed mixed combat. This is a by-product of the mixed martial arts of our students, who are trained experts of various arts. Some of my own students are deep in mixing MMA fighting with the sticks, in conjunction with moves of Balintawak Eskrima techniques as basis of their full contact rambles, still using pads in workouts. I am a passive observer watching the young and the strong flirting with pain and danger.

Like literature, painting, dance and music, eskrima is an art and a science of grace, precision, speed, strength and beauty. I would rather keep it that way. Although clad in violence, martial artists seldom resort to violence. They understand that violence could be deadly and fatal— hardly a price to be paid for an affront, insult or provocation. Besides, the mere study and practice of it are a release of internal aggression and hostility. On the lighter side, most martial artists are henpecked and hectored husbands. They certainly cannot hit or use force and violence against a termagant and shrewish wife. I confess – I cannot and will not hit my wife. Discretion is the better part of valor – walk away. Okay gang: spare me from your wrath!

Eskrima like all martial arts is a great responsibility in the hands of the master. A deadly art should never be taught to irresponsible, violent, ill-tempered brutes, thugs and bullies. Greater care must be taken to keep it from the criminally minded. In the wake of world terrorism, be careful that you are not training future terrorists who would use their skills for evil. This is a late concern for me, seeing the brutality viciousness and callous inhumanity of terrorists. If they are trained with our skills, they will be even more vicious and unmerciful. When starting out to learn, they will come as sheep and be subservient until they don't need you. Be very vigilant and even suspicious.

Eskrima should be used to defend the oppressed and not to oppress the weak and defenseless. It may be added that in this day of guns, it is never wise to swagger and abuse your skills because guns are great equalizers. It does not take much size, strength or training to be at par with the best martial artist. It is best to be soft-spoken, unpretentious and humble about your skills in martial arts. Also remember, it is an art and a manly sport—although concomitantly a deadly means of self-preservation. In olden times, it was a means of survival. In some of our streets, it still is, if you are caught in certain places, situations and circumstances that require its use to protect yourself and your family from harm. After all, someone once said, "There are no second places in street fights." It is not pretty and it is not fair. Thus some advice, "Do not get into a fight but if you must, hit first and hit hard and get out." Never underestimate your opponent. The guy with all the tough looking tattoos may not even know how to throw a punch. He may be making up in appearances what he lacks in skill. Beware of that scrawny little fellow; he may be the better trained fighter or resolute killer. It is to be hoped that, you good people, will never be challenged to use your art during these more civilized times. Unfortunately, there are still uncivilized people who roam our streets that may summon its use. This is when you summon your warrior and survivalist instincts.

Today, eskrimadors are bigger, stronger, and multi-talented with black belts and cross training in other martial arts. I find that among my students and I am sure all the Philippine trained eskrimadors will find that true among their own students. We have some secrets and they want to learn it. As I have said, the mark of a true teacher is the desire to develop students that will turn out better than them and develop the art and the skills even farther. My students still cling to Balintawak Eskrima and acknowledge that they are applying my eskrima principles in their fighting and have improved their own art and eskrima with their multi-faceted skills.

Sadly, those with the least knowledge are the most eager ones to try their skills. This is known as the "green belt mentality" that I have addressed earlier. Be careful in working out with people from other arts or other eskrima styles that come to test you. Beware of treachery. Our grandmaster always warned us against the ruthless and treacherous (matrero). Martial artists are, by nature, probably more paranoid than most people are, always defensive against attack and treachery. That is the nature of the art. In working out in your club, guard against hurting your partner. Mutually learn during your workouts. Again, the nature of the beast involves occasional accidents. Do not take things personally. In sparring with outsiders and strangers, be sure to define the nature of the workout. Will it be controlled or full contact fight? Act accordingly! Be on the alert as even in a controlled workout, the situation can quickly turn nasty into heated full contact combat. Do not be treacherous and correspondingly, do not be a victim of treachery.

Eskrima is effective as a self-defense system for the young, women and the elderly. Again, think of eskrima as an art, and then you will enjoy it for its sophistication, grace and techniques rather than for its violence and brutality. Think of it as an exercise that may extend your life a bit. Use it as a form of fellowship and brotherhood among your fellow enthusiasts. Use it to build self-confidence, character, humility, cool-headed calmness and composure in the face of conflict and hostility. My teaching involves responsibility with the use of this skill.

Enjoy your study, be safe and have fun! Remember, it is an art! Also, remember from whom you learned it. Do not steal and hijack techniques and call them your own. I do not care for material reward but I demand respect, gratitude, allegiance and loyalty to the art, to the masters and to your teachers, and that includes me, if I am your teacher.

Personal Thoughts

From an old man's perch, with a lifetime of unnecessary conflicts and folly, I say: avoid conflict. Conflict does arise and you don't want it; your space is invaded, you are threatened and you are upset, fearful and angry and your adrenalin is pumping. Control your emotions. Lower your decibel. Consider your personal benefits and loses. Is it worth the trouble, really? Ask yourself these questions: "Can I walk away and feel proud of my self-control, knowing that with my skills I can hurt the aggressor? Would I be a 'bigger man' if I could avoid conflict?"

Lower your voice not in fear but with firmness of one who is confident but not hostile. Okay, so you know self-defense. Think of it as a cultural experience, an exercise, a bonding with friends of similar interest, a confidence builder and not as a tool for hostility and belligerence. Besides, someone will be bigger, stronger, faster and better trained than you and many will try to see how good you really are—just like the fastest gunman in the Wild West. Keep your skills to yourself! Besides, this is the age of guns and guns are the great equalizers. And as they used to say in the old country, "It takes only one bullet." With that dark, somber and cryptic warning, cool down and be prudent in your use of strength. I have discussed the legal consequences earlier.

Tips for a Longer Life

Remember:

- Do not carry a chip on your shoulder and dare people to knock it; they will.
- Do not insult people.
- Do not threaten people.
- Stay out of dangerous places and dangerous situations.
- Sometimes violence happens even to nice people; recognize it if and when it happens.
- Provide the other person a face-saving withdrawal.
- Street fights are not fair.
- Be ready and alert.
- Make self-defense your last and final option. Again, there are legal consequences and they can be severe.
- "Jury proof" yourself.
- Be sure you have witnesses hearing your refusal to fight. If you must fight, hit first, hit hard and leave before the cavalry arrives. They will beat you up or worse they may kill you.

Expectations

A question has been asked, what I expect in return for all the free lessons I have given on eskrima. Nothing material. Gratitude and respect count for me. Always remember the people you met on your way up. They will be the same people you will meet on your way down. Gratitude is written on a stone tablet in the Filipino culture. Remember from whom you learned the art and give credit and acknowledgment to your mentors. I have given credit and honor to my mentors, stable mates and most of all to my Grandmaster for the knowledge and skills I have learned from them. Also remember to credit the Balintawak Eskrima system and do not coopt it as belonging to your other style. Share your knowledge and wisdom unselfishly. It was given to you freely. Share it unselfishly. Teach. Teaching is the secret to reinforcing and fortifying your own knowledge and training. If you cannot teach it, that means you have not learned nor understood it enough to explain and teach it. As for respect, respect those who have been generous with their knowledge. I am not particular about the bowing ceremonies, it was a part of our tradition but addressing your teacher must have an element of respect and deference. For me personally, it is sufficient to be addressed as *guro'* for teacher, *manong for elder* or *kuya* for an elder brother. It is not uncommon for Filipinos to address close friends of the family as uncle or *tito*. The title of grandmaster should not be self-anointed but an earned respect given by students and colleagues for those who have earned it in service to the art in terms of its spread worldwide through teaching or publication.

"It's all in the left hand".

Sam with a determined look at 78, old and grizzled. Still in bright colors yet looking to the future though dark glasses wondering if someone will pick up the slack.

Tree of Knowledge

Like the Tree of Knowledge in Genesis, you will start to possess knowledge for good or evil. You will possess dangerous skills that can be tempting and can be abused. Use your skills for noble, upright and righteous causes. Never teach it to the violent, evil and criminally minded. Practice and train hard, practice and train correctly and stay healthy and stay out of trouble! Good luck!

Who Inherits the Mantle of Responsibility for the Buot Legacy?

Grandchildren black belts Christian and Tianna flying like eagles

Christian Samuel Buot – he can fly

Senior student Master Craig Roland Smith

Ryan doing high kicks for posterity

Ryan with a trove of medals and trophies at 11. 5-17-06

The Buot Eskrima Soaring Eagles – Nick Thompson, Ryan Benjamin Buot, Sam Buot, Adam Tompkins, Bart Vermilya and Craig Roland Smith

Buot Balintawak Group 11-22-14

CONCLUSION

Eskrima is a very sophisticated, highly refined, ancient and indigenous art dating to prehistoric Philippines. The ancients seemed to understand the movement of the human body. The human anatomy and movements of the human body have remained unchanged. Thus, the movements of the human body and hand techniques involved in eskrima are largely universal and similar to other martial arts without any conscious efforts of imitating one another. As I have insisted, eskrima is an art all its own. It is not a rehash, make-over or imitation of any other foreign art. While it has evolved with the infusion of moves from students of other arts, eskrima is indeed and, in fact, indigenous to the Philippines. It is growing with the addition of techniques from a family of worldwide practitioners. Today, it is taught to law enforcement officers worldwide and other martial arts schools are including it in their curriculum. Established martial artists have embraced it and mastered it and even improved on it. Many movies have shown Eskrima in fight scenes. Eskrima is no longer a secret.

Balintawak today is different worldwide than it was in its early years in the Philippines, even among those who were touched directly by Anciong Bacon, Jose Villasin, Teofilo Velez and Teddy Buot. Each has developed his own style with his own innovations depending of his own influences, his own studies and research and what he caught and learned during his training and later experience. All in all, there remains basic peculiarities and distinction that is patently and indisputably Balintawak. Like children of the same father and mother, we mold ourselves according to our own influences and training and become our individual and different person, yet in a way there are genetic characteristics that are irrefutably Balintawak.

Balintawak and eskrima in general have grown in geometric proportions. New masters have incorporated old ideas, rehashed them, replenished them and matched them to the new generation of mixed martial arts. It is judicious for us the passing generation to be aware and be accepting of such evolutionary change.

A martial artists as a rule does not or should not start a fight; however, he may defend against an aggressor before counter-attacking. This does not mean that a martial artist should always be on the defensive, nor does it mean that he should always wait for an attack. Personally, as a shorter man, if in my judgment the attack is imminent, I will strike first with a caveat that I would make sure that people observing or watching know that I did not want a fight nor did I start the fight. I will announce out loud that I do not want a fight and raise my hands as if in surrender. This move is a ready and offensive move for the slightest flicker of a move on an opponent's part. This is similar to the Muay Thai ready position.

I have explained my philosophy of martial arts, the art of controlled violence, to my sons and my students. I told them that martial arts and physical strength was the first line by which men gained respect from other men—physical strength, power and physical superiority. That is the law of the jungle—the Darwinian "survival of the fittest"—respect for the biggest, fiercest and strongest among them. The next level of respect among men is their respect for intelligence, knowledge and intellectual superiority—the doctors, lawyers, engineers, scientists, inventors and creators. Then they respected the power of material wealth of the builders, industrialists, manufacturers and creators of wealth as a confirmation of that superior intellect and leadership. The fourth is their respect for moral courage, goodness, wisdom and integrity. If wealth and power are earned through foul means they will lose all that power and authority. They may even be shamed and land in jail. The men who will have lasting respect and honor in the pantheons of the Gods will be the righteous men, the men of integrity and men of wisdom. Try to be all of those men. Eskrima and physical strength are only the first step, an important step to being an all-around or Renaissance man.

APPENDIX

THE BALINTAWAK FAMILY TREE

This list may start a controversy as many will claim direct tutelage under the grandmaster and as pure students of Anciong. Others will claim the Balintawak banner and claim tutelage under the Grandmaster despite the fact they may not even been borne before he passed away. There is truth to the fact that Bacon did in fact tour the various clubs to check the students of Villasin and Velez and possibly had other private students. It is hard to say whether or not they were pure students since they were tutored by different masters which from time to time may have been visited by Bacon. Initially, Bacon felt that these splinter groups were competitors to him, albeit the teachers were his students. These students, though, claimed allegiance to him. In a large city where transportation was not readily available to poorer students, they had to learn from the source closest to them. This was true as in the case of the Villasin-Velez Group which was largely in the Pari-an District. The Maranga group was in the Pasil District.

Below is a list of the major direct students of Grandmaster Anciong Bacon. Under each of their names, is the list of those who studied or were promoted under them. One can see from here, who studied with whom, and keep the stories straight. First is the lineage chart of direct students of Anciong, followed by listings of students under each master. More detailed information on each of the leading masters found here is provided in *Chapter 2: Masters of Balintawak*.

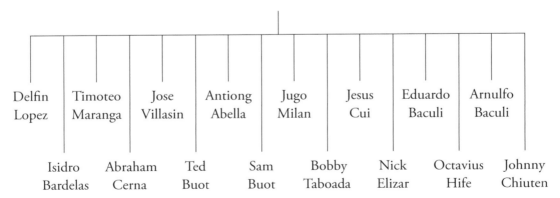

**Venancio "Anciong" Bacon
(Founder of Balintawak)**

Delfin Lopez	Timoteo Maranga	Jose Villasin	Antiong Abella	Jugo Milan	Jesus Cui	Eduardo Baculi	Arnulfo Baculi
	Isidro Bardelas	Abraham Cerna	Ted Buot	Sam Buot	Bobby Taboada	Nick Elizar	Octavius Hife	Johnny Chiuten

DELFIN LOPEZ
David Paez, Bebe Paez, Inting Atillo, Jody Lopez

TIMOTEO MARANGA
Rodrigo "Drigo" Maranga, Arnulfo "Toto" Moncal, Remy Presas

JOSE VILLASIN
Teofilo Velez, Tinong Ybanez, Bianor Villasin, Ver Villasin, Joey Villasin, Sam Buot

TED BUOT
Cebu Group: Arturo Sanchez, Leodegario "Ludy" Ocanada, Irvin Ocanada, Emmanuel "Boyet" Hife, Dr. Antonio Abella, Doming Zabala, Ernie Reyes, Fred Buot, Jr., Sam Buot, Esperidion "Edion" dela Cerna, Rencio, Octavius "Jimboy" Hife

USA Group: Rocky Pasiwk, Ricky Casquejo, Mani' Cabase, Erwin Ballarta, Conrado Garcia, Steve Acho, Ken Kershaw, David Hatch, Lance de Vought, Manuel Reynoso, Jaye Spiro, Kevin Rothowski, Jim Gomez, Mike Power, Wayne Wells, Mark Favazza, Manny Cabase, Jacob Ketterwell, Mike Cribbs, Tim Hartman, Rich Parsons, Richard Cotteril

SAM BUOT
Larry Vasquez, Mike Worden, David Buot, Orville Turner, Bart Vermilya, Craig Smith, Allen Sandoval, Joe Staszkow, John Jacobo, Kim Essendrup, Don Hattery, Ryan Buot, Rob Casquejo, Ramiel Ignacio, Adam Tompkins, Frank Spangler, Nick Thompson, Jon Buot, Sal Banuelos, Bob Harris, Leonard Meuerer, Thiel Ruperto, Carlos Sevilla, Danny Sevilla, Mark Cañez, Paul Bannon, Jun Saguid, Matt Yeoman, Angelina Berenkova, Audie Batita, Greg Trent, Leonard "Leny" de Fusco, Danny Corpuz, Gallant Betita, Glenn Bennett

BOBBY TABOADA
Bobby Taboada has branches and the most extensive number of students worldwide in the USA, England, Scotland, Austria, Switzerland, and Poland. Representatives can be found on his website WorldBalintawak.com

OCTAVIUS HIFE
Cary Sanchez, Celso Caballero, Edward Caballero, Geronimo "Itchuy" Brizo, Gregorio "Gorio" Jaymar, Octavio "Taby" Lim, Rolando "Boy" Oropeo, Ruben Rizon, Bebot, Nonilon "Nilon" Abella, Atty. Tirso "Sonny" Ferrer, Jr., Rhett Cambonga Ferrer, Ramon (the salakat guy), Ramon (the baker guy), "lstan" (the rice cake vendor), Nuy Drico, Capt. Benjamin Martinez Monzon, Amanda Manman Tian, Capt. Johnny Tanco Pintoy, Capt. Albino Collantes, Capt. Von Sunga, Capt. Hilario Villanueva, Franco Guerrero, Kieren John Hife, Remberto "Bebe" Fernandez, Ethan Buot Frakes, Capt. Avelino "Billy" Samuya

TEOFILO VELEZ
Dr. Ben Marapao, Winnie de la Cruz, Romy de la Cruz, Nonato "Nene" Gaabucayan, Nick Elizar, Nilo Servila, Chito Velez, Bobby Tabimina

GLOSSARY

abecedario - (n) ABC's., that is the teaching of basics.

agak - (v) To teach, coach or tutor; *Inagak* (n) student; *Gui-agak* (v) tutored.

Aikido - (n) A Japanese form of martial arts, utilizing, wrist, joints and elbow grips to immobilize an opponent.

amakan - (n) Latticed bamboo walls.

amara - (n & v) A fancy manipulation of the stick mostly for intimidation, show or exercise.

arnis - (n) Martial arts of the Philippines, also known as eskrima, kalirongan, garote, baston, kuntao, silat, gilas, pagkalikali, panandata, didya, kabaroan, kaliradman, sinawali.

badlong - (v & adj) To rebuke, reprimand, scold or stop rude behavior.

bahad - (n & v) Full contact duel, often to the finish or until one combatant begs to be spared.

bakbakan or ***bogbogan*** – (n & v) Fighting or beating each other.

Balintawak - (n) Balintawak is a place in Caloocan, Rizal, known as Pugadlawin, where the patriot Andres Bonifacio made his famous cry for an armed struggle in revolt against Spain. This was later known as later *Sigaw ng Pugadlawin* ("cry from the eagle's nest"). It is also a side street in Cebu City, where a style of eskrima, created by Grandmaster Venancio "Anciong" Bacon had its humble beginnings.

bali-bali - (v) Literally meaning "flip-flop," reversing strikes, as used in eskrima.

balisong - (n) A fan knife made in the Philippines, mostly in the province of Batangas.

balitok - (v) Flip, reverse.

bangga' - (v) Bump, also, a contest, battle, match or competition

banig - (n) Training mat.

bansay - (n) Able, ready and trained.

baston - (n) Refers to the eskrima stick, also known as olisi, hapak or bunal'.

barang - (n) Curse or to cast a curse or magic spell

berada - (adj) The act of pulling the stick back before delivering a strike, usually to gain momentum or power. We also call it chambering.

bikil or bingki - (n & v) A confrontation, argument, disagreement.

bokbokanay - (v & adj) Beating each other or fierce fighting.

bud-hi - (adj & n) Treachery, deceit, betrayal, ruthlessness and trickery.

bugno' - (v or n) To wrestle, grapple; syn: *dumog, layug.*

bunal' - (v) To strike or beat; (n) an instrument used to strike, mostly referring to the eskrima stick as a striking weapon; syn: *puspos, hapak.*

bu'no - (n) Fight to death or duel ending in death; (v) to kill.

busdak or bundak - (n & v) To slam down, bang down or drop down.

cabra - (v) A ripping strike or thrust, leading with the point of the stick.

corridas - (n) Spanish for bullfight, also means fast and without stopping. In eskrima, it is used to mean successive random strikes without stopping and in succession. Some use it to mean striking un-choreographed strikes or random strikes.

corto - (n & v) Derived from a Spanish word, meaning short, which in Balintawak Eskrima is used to mean an abbreviated or truncated strike to the hand, usually when the hand is unnecessarily extended making it an easy target.

coupe de grace - A French word pronounced as ku da gras, meaning blow of mercy.

daga - (n) Spanish for dagger, the Cebuano word for dagger is *baraw* and sometimes called *balaraw.*

dagat - (n & adj) It could mean the sea or sea-sick, depending on the accent or use.

dakdak - (v & adj) To bash, smash or slam down.

dasmag or hasmag - (v) To rush into or ram or smash into.

dawat - (v) Literally,to receive, accept or catch as in catching a pass or a strike

dunggab or duslak, tuslak - (v) To stab vs. *duslak, tuslak* meaning to thrust with a pointed object, like a knife or sword.

Doce Pares - (n) One of the dominant eskrima styles in Cebu, meaning "twelve pairs" allegedly from Charlemagne.

dumog - (v) Grapple, wrestle or tackle. Syn: *layug, bugno'.*

eskrima - (n) See *Arnis.*

gunting - (n) Scissors or (v) to cut with scissors or a scissors technique.

guro' - (n) Teacher; *punong-guro* meaning head teacher - In Cebuano, sometimes the Spanish word *maestro* is used or the purist Cebuano's call them *magtutudlo'* or *tig-agak*.

hapak* or *bunal' - (n) A striking weapon or (v) to strike.

hata' - (v) A fake or a deceptive ploy or ruse to create an opening or entry into an opponent's position such as doing a head fake or faking a strike.

herbolario - (n) Herbal doctors, medicine men, or quack doctors.

hikap -(v & n) to touch, feel and sense the direction, presence or absence of pressure.

hilot - (n) Art of Filipino massage; *manghihilot*, masseuse.

hubad - (v & adj) Untangle or untie.

iyahay - (n & v) Sparring independently free from control or guidance. This means the instructor no longer controls you and you don't allow yourself to be controlled. This is advanced fighting stage where each applies *kwentada*, ruses, subterfuges and deceptions to get your strike or technique through.

juego todo - (v & n) Spanish, meaning to play or to gamble all; in eskrima meaning to hit with full force and power in full contact.

juramentado - (n) A frenzied and violent rage, actually from the Spanish word *juramentar*, meaning one who takes an oath. In this case, they referred to a Muslim warrior, who takes an oath to kill Christians often leading to his own death, similar to today's suicide bombers. This is different from *amok* or *amuck* which is a Malay word for uncontrolled rage. Both words have been used interchangeably in the Philippines.

kabya, kablig or ***sablig*** (v & n) Splashing, tossing or throwing water with a cup or by hand; used to denote the move of tossing the opponent's hand to the opposite side of the body.

kagis - (v & n) to scrape, scratch, grade or cause abrasion.

kawras or ***kamras*** - (v) to scratch or scrape usually with the nails on the face or eyes.

kali - (n) The term kali is more widely used in the US and is gaining wider use in the Philippines, popularized by the dean of martial artists, Dan Inosanto, of the Bruce Lee fame. Rural areas in the Philippines may have never heard of it.

kalit - (v) sudden, snap, abrupt, unforeseen and unexpected.

karateka - (n) A practitioner of karate.

kata - (n) Dances or exercises in Japanese martial arts that simulate attacks and defenses.

kempetai - (n) Brutal Japanese military police, well noted for torture and cruelty.

kung-fu - (n) A Chinese martial art based on fluid movements of arms and legs.

ku-ot - (v) To reach in or dig in stealthily.

kusog - (n, adj & v) Usually refers to speed or strength, depending on the use of the word.

kwentada - (n & v) the etymology or root comes from the Spanish word cuenta meaning to count or calculate, as used in eskrima meaning, a ruse by making a move or strike calculated to lure or entice a counter-move feeding into a swift and lethal counter-strike.

labnot - (n & v) To pull or yank in a sudden, swift, and jerking manner.

labtik, witik or **pitik** - (n & v) To snap back like a rubber band, usually referring to the flick or whipping strike, sometimes a fan strike or abaniko.

labyug - (n & v) To swing, sway or oscillate.

latigo - (n & v) Spanish, meaning whip.

layug - (v & n) to wrestle, grapple often used interchangeably with *dumog*.

lansis - (n) A ruse, subterfuge or ploy to deceive and entrap the opponent into a pre-planned offensive move.

largo mano - (n & adj) Adapted from Spanish, literally to let go of your arm or long distance fighting.

liguat - (v) to pry open as in using a lever and fulcrum.

ligas - (v) to slip, evade, elude or dodge.

likay or **lihay** - (v) to dodge, elude, escape or evade.

lubid or **pisi** - (n) Rope, sometimes the word *pisi* is sometimes used. It is also used, meaning to twist or wind likes a rope.

maestro - (n) Spanish, meaning teacher or *magtutudlo'* or *tig-agak* in Cebuano or *guro'* in Tagalog.

maharlika - (n) Royal blood, nobility or royal family, rooted in ancient Indian Sanskrit, the word *mahardikha*, meaning a man of wealth.

manong or **manoy** - (n or adj) Terms of respect for an older male, oftentimes address to an older brother, cousin or just any one older. Sometimes contraction of the words such as *'Nong, 'Noy* and *Mano* are used.

matrero - (n) Treacherous, cunning, sly and with intent on foul or unfair play.

moro-moro - (n) A socio-political play or performance showing the Moros (native Muslims) as pagans and villains.

musmus, mudmud or *bagnud* - (v) to push or rub an opponent's face on the ground,

olisi - (n) A synonym for eskrima stick, also known as *baston, hapak* or *bunal'*.

pa-ak, kagat or *hangbat* - (v) to bite.

pa-apas or pagukod - (n & v) A gambit that forces the opponent to chase, pursue or defend against a strike; again, a form of ruse and entrapment strategy.

pa-awas - (n & v) flow-over or spill-over, as in parrying a strike.

pabanda or *pa-untol* - (n & v) to bounce back or spring back.

padungan - (n & v) it is a simultaneous strike. The root word is *dungan*, meaning, together.

pahulog - (n) to allow a drop or fall.

pakalit - (n) Sudden, quick, rapid and swift strikes.

pakung or *pakang* - (n) to bump as in bumping the head.

palabtik - (n) the root word being labtik, meaning snap back - a snapping fulcrum strike.

palakat - (n) Un-choreographed and random defense and offense or walk-through the different strike angles and defenses.

palaway - (n) to tempt, entice, bait or deceive the opponent, as in a ruse or subterfuge. Literally meaning, to allow a person to salivate or drool over what appears as an open strike.

palipat - (n) this is a sleight of hand or a deft and deceptive move used on the theory that "the hand is quicker than the eye".

palis - (n) to open up, to clear, to unveil and expose. Sometimes the word sapwang is used interchangeably. Sometimes the word KABYA would be used.

palusot - (n & v) to allow one to hit or strike unopposed. To sneak a strike unopposed or unblocked or to hit through. The root word is lusot, meaning to go through unopposed and unimpeded.

pamatid - (n) Visayan for kicking skills; the root word is patid, meaning to kick. Another synonym would be sikad.

pamislit - (n) Art of using pressure points; the root word is pislit, meaning to press or squeeze.

pana' - (n, v) an arrow or the act of hunting with a bow and arrow or fishing with a fishing tool consisting of an arrow powered by rubber band or mechanical power.

pang-agaw - (v) Disarming, snatching and take-away techniques

panumba - (n) Breaking opponent's balance; the root word is tumba, meaning to fall down

pa-on - (n) Bait, tempts, induce or lure

patagak (kan) - (n & v) to allow the stick to fall or drop on the opponent's leg, using his own momentum or pressure.

patay - (n, adj. or v) Depending on the placement of the accent, it could mean dead or to duel and fight to death or kill.

patid/sikad/sipa' (n & v) Kick.

payong - (n) Umbrella also meaning the umbrella defense or simulating an umbrella (with the butt of the stick up and the point down.

paypay - (n) Fan or fan strike, characterized by flipping the stick in a fan-like movement by wrist action also known as abanico.

pok-pok - (n & v) to pound or hit with the butt of the stick. The other term is puño, as in the handle of the stick.

pugadlawin - n) In Tagalog, it *pugad* means nest and *lawin*, means eagle or eagle's nest.

puño - (n) A Spanish word, meaning handle, fist or cuff. (n) Cebuano pokpok means using the butt of the stick in an offensive move as in butting.

redondo - (v & n) it is both a style of eskrima and a style of striking, which is the whipping style through fan-like wrist twists.

sa'sa' - (n & v) To batter, beat or pummel, more particularly referring to the use of the stick by sliding it down on the hand to slash or hack the hand.

sagang - (v, n) Defense or to defend

sagbay - (n & v) to sling or fling on the shoulder

sablig or ***kabya*** - (v) to throw cast or splash water or liquid especially from a vessel or pot. It is often meant to cast the opponent's hand and/or stick to the other side.

sangka - (v) Contact or crossing of the sticks; to clash or BANGGA

sapwang - (v) To scoop up or lift up.

seguida - (n) The term is borrowed from the Spanish word *seguidas*, meaning continuance, pursuit, at once, or in succession or immediately. This has been used in lieu of *palakat*, meaning the non-choreographed strikes and counterstrikes.

Sikaran - (n & v) To fight by kicking or use of the foot. This is mostly a Tagalog term.

siko - (n & v) Elbow used as a noun or as a verb. It could mean an elbow strike.

sinawali - (n) A dance-like motions with or without sticks – also a religious dance disguising martial arts dance movements. It is a style of eskrima using two sticks in a weaving pattern after the word sawali, which is split bamboo slats woven in a pattern and used for walls in some Filipino homes.

sipit - (n & v) Clip, as in clipping under the armpit or with the fingers; syn: *kumpit, lugpit.*

solo baston - (n) Single stick.

sumpit - (n) Blow-pipe.

sungag - (v) To meet or hit head-on, usually an anticipated strike met with an open palm in a pre-emptive manner.

suntok - (n & v) To box or punch synonymous with *sumbag.*

suntokan - (v) Boxing, mostly a Tagalog term adapted by Cebuanos. Cebuanos use the term *sumbagay.*

sumbag - (v) Cebuano word meaning to box or punch.

sumbagay - (v) Boxing or fighting.

supo - (v) To blunt a strike in anticipation of its full force.

suyop - (v) To suck in, pull in or absorb, as in absorbing a strike or punch.

tabas - (v) To slice or cut.

Tagalog - (n) Philippine national language predominantly spoken in the Manila region.

takilid - (v) Turn side-wise as an evasive move for a thrust (tostada).

tanday - (v & adj) Lay on as in an arm or fist laid on top opponent's hand to gain control and feel for his moves.

tigbas - (n & v) To hack or slash, as with a bolo.

tukas or **tukwas** - (v & avd) To open up and clear usually referring to the move when sticks are crossed, the action is to clear your opponent's stick by holding or clearing it with the back of your hand to open up the stick for a strike.

tuhod - (n, v) Knee or the act of striking with the knee.

tumba - (v) To break balance or to fall.

tumbada - (adj) Inclined or tilted, as in a tilted stick.

tumba-tumba - (adj) To tumble, flip-flop or to tilt to one side, then to the other

tuslok - (v, n) To thrust or to poke with a pointed object vs. *dunggab, duslak* - to stab.

tapi-tapi - (v) Hand checks by swatting strikes.

tatay - (n) Father.

to-ok or *lo-ok* – (v) To choke or to strangle.

totsada - (v) Thrust.

unay - (v, adj) To be hit with your own weapon or to hurt yourself or to self-inflict.

uway - (n) Rattan.

undayag - (v) To weave and sway.

visayan (bisaya) - (n, adj) Natives of the Visayan Islands.

witik or *labtik* - (v,) To snap back or a quick snap strike.

TAMBULI MEDIA

Excellence in Mind-Body Health & Martial Arts Publishing

Welcome to Tambuli Media, publisher of quality books on mind-body martial arts and wellness presented in their cultural context.

Our Vision is to see quality books once again playing an integral role in the lives of people who pursue a journey of personal development, through the documentation and transmission of traditional knowledge of mind-body cultures.

Our Mission is to partner with the highest caliber subject-matter experts to bring you the highest quality books on important topics of health and martial arts that are in-depth, well-written, clearly illustrated and comprehensive.

Tambuli is the name of a native instrument in the Philippines fashioned from the horn of a carabao. The tambuli was blown and its sound signaled to villagers that a meeting with village elders was to be in session, or to announce the news of the day. It is hoped that Tambuli Media publications will "bring people together and disseminate the knowledge" to many.

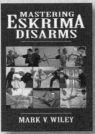

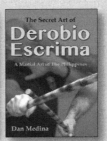
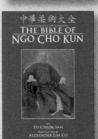

www.TambuliMedia.com

Made in the USA
San Bernardino, CA
28 February 2015